Praise for
AARP Love and Meaning After 50

"A must-read for anyone over fifty who is married or wants to be. I wish my parents had read this book when they were in their fifties! It's a practical, hopeful guide to renegotiating and reinvigorating your relationships. It will save a lot of marriages, because it will really help you and your spouse talk to each other."

—**Stephen Fried,** *New York Times* bestselling author of *Husbandry: Sex, Love, and Dirty Laundry—Inside the Minds of Married Men* and *Rush: Revolution, Madness, and the Visionary Doctor Who Became a Founding Father*

"A beautifully written guide for couples who want inspiration, a refresher, or a reboot after the kids are gone."

—**William J. Doherty, Ph.D.**, Professor of Family Social Science, University of Minnesota, and author of *Take Back Your Marriage*

"Julia Mayer and Barry Jacobs have given us an eminently practical guide to maintaining connection and re-establishing intimacy for couples over fifty. They provide engaging descriptions and clear, step-by-step guidance to help couples forge deeper meaning and greater closeness. As the percentage of Americans over sixty-five continues to grow, this will become an increasingly important and relevant book for an ever-larger segment of our population."

—**Dr. Patricia Papernow,** author of *Surviving and Thriving in Stepfamily Relationships: What Works and What Doesn't* and, with Karen Bonnell, *The Stepfamily Handbook: From Dating to Getting Serious to Forming a "Blended Family"*

Love and Meaning
After 50

Real Possibilities

Love and Meaning After 50

The 10 Challenges to Great Relationships—
and How to Overcome Them

JULIA L. MAYER, PSY.D.
BARRY J. JACOBS, PSY.D.

hachette
BOOKS
New York

Copyright © 2020 by Julia L. Mayer and Barry J. Jacobs. All rights reserved. AARP is a registered trademark.
Cover design by Amanda Kain
Cover photograph © Hero Images
Cover copyright © 2020 by Hachette Book Group, Inc.

Hachette Book Group supports the right to free expression and the value of copyright. The purpose of copyright is to encourage writers and artists to produce the creative works that enrich our culture.

The scanning, uploading, and distribution of this book without permission is a theft of the author's intellectual property. If you would like permission to use material from the book (other than for review purposes), please contact permissions@hbgusa.com. Thank you for your support of the author's rights.

Hachette Go, an imprint of Hachette Books
Hachette Book Group
1290 Avenue of the Americas
New York, NY 10104
HachetteGo.com
Facebook.com/HachetteGo
Instagram.com/HachetteGo

First Edition: August 2020

Hachette Books is a division of Hachette Book Group, Inc.
The Hachette Go and Hachette Books name and logos are trademarks of Hachette Book Group, Inc.
The publisher is not responsible for websites (or their content) that are not owned by the publisher.

Print book interior design by Jeff Williams

Library of Congress Cataloging-in-Publication Data has been applied for.
ISBNs: 978-0-7382-8618-1 (paperback); 978-0-7382-8617-4 (e-book)

Printed in the United States of America

LSC-C

10 9 8 7 6 5 4 3 2 1

Contents

Introduction

One day, about seven years ago, we found ourselves looking at each other in frustration in our too-quiet house. We'd just had an unproductive argument over something irrelevant that neither of us can even remember now. What was obvious was that, after twenty-three years of marriage, we both felt alone and discontented. That was when, as two psychologists with more than fifty years of professional experience between us, we recognized that we had a problem.

It had begun three years before, when our daughter turned eighteen and left for college and we'd had to adjust to having just our son at home. We missed the spontaneous conversations with our daughter, taking care of her in small ways like preparing meals she enjoyed, listening to her concerns, and even giving her cash to hang out with her friends. With our son's departure three years later to a school even farther away, we grew more unsettled. We realized that beneath our pride in our children's accomplishments, we were grieving those rewarding, painful, joyful, intense, exhausting, exhilarating years of raising our children. We found ourselves feeling older and unsure about what would come next.

Fortunately, our professional experience gave us insight into what to do about it. We began to share our feelings, reassess the state of our marriage, and think about the next phase of our lives. We carved out time in our busy schedules to talk and listen to each other so that we could share what each of us hoped for in this new phase of our lives.

We discovered that checking in with each other just a few minutes each day helped. A dinner out or a walk around the neighborhood usually renewed our feelings of connection, regardless of the stressors of the day. We started traveling together, just the two of us, for the first time in years. We went to dinner with other couples more frequently. We leaned on each other more emotionally and planned together for our new life ahead. We slowly adapted to our quieter, more predictable life.

In time, we decided to bring new energy to our relationship by developing new mutual interests. When the opportunity to write our first book together arose, we saw it as a way for us to transition to becoming couple-focused again. That was *AARP Meditations for Caregivers: Practical, Emotional, and Spiritual Support for You and Your Family*, published in 2016, where we shared our own and others' experiences as caregivers—we cared for both of our parents over the years—giving us the chance to process our feelings about our journey and loss while strengthening our relationship.

Nowadays, when our children come home, we find their visits a bit disruptive to the new life we have created. In a strange way, it's like having houseguests who feel comfortable eating everything in sight and using every towel in the house. We love it and them, and we experience renewed sadness when they leave again. But we are also, honestly, a little relieved. We can get back to our now familiar and satisfying empty-nest marital routine.

We are far from alone in our marital struggles at this stage of life. Empty nest, caregiving, loss: These and other challenges affect couples over fifty. Some don't survive; the rate of divorce is rising. We come from a cohort of Americans—the baby boomers—who divorce more than any generation before or since.

We were lucky; we had years of experience to help us find our way. But most couples over fifty have no road map for how to cope. They need a path for this unique stage to strengthen their romantic relationships. Thus, the idea for this, our second book, came together.

Couples over fifty are qualitatively different from the untested infatuations and child-focused partnerships earlier in life. Happy and healthy long-standing relationships of mature couples are largely based on the hard-won sense of security and mutual values, acceptance, and admiration that frequently come with long years of joy and struggle together. When the kids are more or less launched, there is less family responsibility, so we turn more toward our reliable and trustworthy partners to nurture us, enjoy the present, share our memories of the past, and create a common dream for the future.

Mostly, this time in our lives is full of opportunity. Americans over fifty are in many ways prospering. Our ability to live longer, healthier lives is one of science's great achievements. With these bonus years, we work later in life—by choice or need—and travel more than ever before. The increased average life span of today's Americans gives them more options to end their marriages and to flex their wings and take off—a choice that couples in unsatisfying relationships from shorter-lived previous generations didn't have. We are not willing to settle, waiting out our final decades with dull or dying relationships. We seek loving and meaningful partnerships that last. And we thrive in those relationships. Research has found positive correlations between being married and enjoying better health and greater longevity—as much as a ten-year extension in life span.

How, then, can we help you not just preserve but strengthen your relationship after age fifty? No, it's not to keep you stuck or to settle because you're too old to hold out for true love. That is just not true. Rather, we focus on the steps you need to take to find love, meaning, and fulfillment in your relationship. Or determine if your current marriage really won't bring you what you need. (And a caveat here: You should consider seeking professional help when needed. This book is not a panacea for all marital woes.)

In our practices, we've found ten specific challenges that couples over fifty face that are quite different from those of younger couples. By addressing them, you can strengthen your relationship and redefine who you are together in order to thrive anew. In this book, we explore the challenges one by one:

Challenge 1: The Empty Nest—US couples are often child-centered. When the children grow up and move out, many longtime relationships flounder. How can couples become reacquainted and reinvigorate their relationships?

Challenge 2: Extended Family—Sometimes adult children move back home and need financial and other help. Sometimes other family members need assistance. These demands draw energy and resources away from our partners and can create conflict. How can we balance upholding family responsibilities and caring for each other?

Challenge 3: Finances—For many couples fifty and older, their prime earning years either will end soon or are already behind them. Some are prospering; others plan for belt-tightening. How can they decide together on their spending and saving priorities?

Challenge 4: Infidelity—Unfaithfulness threatens longtime relationships more than other challenges generally do. Surprisingly, infidelity is more common among older couples. The rates of infidelity peak for men in their seventies and for women in their sixties—just when couples are struggling to cope with other changes. How can partners weather the crisis and recommit to improving their relationship?

Challenge 5: Retirement—If having too little time together during the working years can make partners feel neglected by each other, then having too much time together in retirement can make them feel intruded upon. How do we find the right balance between We Time and Me Time? And how do we make this time in our lives productive and meaningful?

Challenge 6: Downsizing and Relocating—Decluttering and moving can be cleansing and open up new opportunities, but it can also be distressing. How can partners agree on when and what to move and then adjust to a new space and new support systems?

Challenge 7: Sex—Intimacy is at the heart of couples' emotional lives. But many partners are uncomfortable discussing a diminishing spark and changing sexual needs. Strengthening feelings of closeness by communicating more openly and adapting to needs and preferences over time can keep couples enjoying closeness in the years ahead.

Challenge 8: Health Concerns—For every adult over fifty who is hitting the gym and eating more salads, three are more sedentary than ever and taking health for granted. Partners need to encourage each other to take better care of themselves for the sake of each other. And to recommit to being there for each other in sickness and in health.

Challenge 9: Caregiving—We get sick, our parents are aging, other relatives and friends get sick. How can partners become ever closer as they face illness and disability together?

Challenge 10: Loss of Loved Ones—Grief within a relationship can bring partners closer or create emotional distance. Can partners commune in sadness and deepen their connection?

At the end of the ten challenges, we've added a section titled "When Nothing Works: Cooperative Separation and Divorce." If you walk through the challenges and still can't strengthen your connection, you may ultimately choose to walk away. We help you decide whether to stay or leave and, if you decide to leave, we help you to do that in a way that honors yourselves, your relationship, and your families.

How to Use This Book

The first half of each challenge is filled with insights and anecdotes from our professional and personal experience along with the latest research and statistics.

The second half walks you through the solution. First, you'll find a relationship Check-Up. You'll each fill out the Check-Up separately and then come together to discuss your responses. There are no rights and wrongs; it's all a process of getting to know each other through talking frankly and listening empathetically. We show you how to do that, step by step. Then we offer a simple but effective process to negotiate these issues and life transitions over the weeks, months, and years ahead. In the next section, you'll find tips for talking and listening, which you can use throughout the process.

Your relationship matters. And it requires care. We'll help you consciously clarify your values and goals and use them together to guide your relationship to greater intimacy and happiness. The choices in this exciting stage of life can be daunting, but when you work together as a couple, carefully listening to each other and sharing your hopes and dreams as well as fears and insecurities, solving problems, and creating meaning, your life will be more rewarding and bring you greater satisfaction. In the best relationships, we create shared senses of purpose and sources of enjoyment and intimacy.

Our goal with this book is to help you use these bonus years to reconstruct your relationship to better fit the dimensions of life after fifty. We hope that refashioning that structure together will bring you comfort, joy, meaning, and love.

—JULIA L. MAYER AND BARRY J. JACOBS

Tips for Talking and Listening

Throughout this book, we suggest you talk and listen to deepen and strengthen your relationship. It's more challenging than you may think. It requires patience and practice.

You aren't solving specific problems during this time; you are sharing feelings and learning about each other.

The couples we work with have found the following guidelines helpful.

1. Make an appointment in advance to talk with each other. Pick a time when you are both likely to feel able to listen and talk at your own pace without pressure.

2. Choose a quiet place where you won't be interrupted or distracted and where you'll feel comfortable and have privacy.

3. Turn off or silence devices if you can.

4. Remember that this likely isn't easy for either of you.

5. Let yourselves be vulnerable.
6. Give your partner time to talk.
7. Do your best to listen patiently, quietly, and openly.
8. Refrain from being critical, judgmental, or defensive.
9. Respond to your partner with validating comments, even if you're feeling surprised or upset. Just listen closely and summarize aloud what you've heard.
10. Be respectful and supportive.

Remember that your goal is to strengthen your connection. This will be an opportunity to feel closer.

Challenge 1

The Empty Nest

Carol leaned toward Julia as if to speak in confidence, though Ben was sitting next to her on the black leather couch in Julia's office. Putting her hand to the side of her mouth, Carol loudly whispered, "I don't know what to do with him."

Their twin daughters had left for college six months earlier, and the couple was sitting in Julia's psychotherapy office because it wasn't going so well.

Ben shrugged and looked uncomfortable. Carol continued: "He sits in front of the TV and watches cable news all day long on the weekends and every night. Or he's on his phone. What are we going to do when he retires? I can't live like this. He doesn't want to go on walks with me or join me when I go shopping." She sighed. "He always spent the weekends doing sports with the girls. It's like life ended for him when they left."

Julia looked over at Ben, who shrugged again before saying morosely, "We have nothing in common. I don't like to take walks, and shopping sounds like torture to me. Either I'm going to the gym or I'm relaxing at home. I don't really know what she wants from me."

Carol responded, "I was hoping, now that you aren't so busy with the girls every weekend, that you and I might spend some time together. I've been waiting for this time. It's not that I don't miss the girls. I do, but I want my marriage back."

Ben said suddenly in a loud, derisive voice, "As if you can magically make that happen. Snap your fingers." He snapped his fingers in her face.

For many couples, the empty nest is a rude awakening. After years of close cooperation with raising children, coordinating chores, and juggling family and work schedules, it can come as a shock when spouses are finally alone together and turn toward each other with a feeling of unfamiliarity. Just as Ben and Carol discovered, the children are no longer there on a day-to-day basis to fill the house with activity and unite the parents in common cause. Instead, in the sudden quiet, uneasiness creeps in. Do the spouses still know each other as people, not just co-parents? Do they love each other as much as they once did? Or was something in their relationship lost through the years of child-focused family life?

Some partners do thrive during the empty-nest stage. After the last child leaves, they are exuberant about the decreased housework and day-to-day responsibilities; the increased opportunities for independent and social activities and self-development; the time for travel, new career pursuits, and hobbies. But for those who flounder through this transition, four main reasons often arise: mishandled emotions, divergence of interests, lack of relationship-building skills, and conflicted family priorities.

Mishandled Emotions

Carol's main complaint about the state of their marriage was that Ben was emotionally distant. All those hours in front of the TV, at work, or in the gym didn't bring him into conversation with her. Rather, his preoccupation with other things felt to her like a withdrawal or even rejection. She could understand that they were a little rusty with talking about their emotions; they'd been talking for so long only about how the kids were coping. But Ben didn't even seem interested in relating to her. They were coexisting, passing each other in the hallways or at the kitchen table without much interaction.

They'd drifted into parallel lives in which they'd devoted so much time and energy to their girls that they'd forgotten to pay attention to each other. Sitting in Julia's office, they seemed awkward even looking at or speaking to each other. Years earlier, they'd stopped sharing feelings that weren't about their children.

For many couples, emotional distance is often spurred by emotional misalignment. One spouse is beset with sadness; the other with anger. One volubly expresses how she feels; the other is stoical and silent. When stress in a marriage increases, including during the empty-nest period, differences in emotional styles become more pronounced. Then both spouses can feel alone with their feelings and convinced that the other spouse is out of touch.

Carol and Ben were misaligned in this way. She missed their children but felt mostly annoyance with him because for years he had hardly talked to her about anything but the girls and never inquired about her. In her mind, he didn't seem to care. Ben did care, at least to a degree, but he was preoccupied. Because the twins, not Carol, had constituted so much of his world, he was now utterly bereft. At Julia's prompting, he admitted he felt dread and sadness, as if his life were dwindling away.

Feelings of grief are not uncommon for the empty-nest transition. For many couples, raising children can be the most meaningful activity they have ever experienced. They may throw themselves into it, savoring every moment of it, relishing their identity as parents. Many enjoy providing emotional support and guidance as their children grow up. They love feeling needed and being able to meet their children's needs. Making favorite meals, throwing parties, or driving carloads of children to activities can feel extremely rewarding to eagerly involved parents. Many become active, valued members of their community by getting involved with their children's education, sports, or activities: offering to serve on the school board, coach a sport, or raise money for costumes for a play. When these roles—which have become so crucial to a parent's self-concept—disappear, that parent may suffer an identity crisis. *What will define me now?* he may ask himself. *What do I have to look forward to that will be as meaningful as raising my children?* The departure of the last child is also a clear signal to parents that they are getting older and must deal with their own aging and disappointments about past hopes and dreams.

Integrating those painful feelings of loss can be a lonely process if the spouses don't feel similarly or if they grieve too differently. There is an opportunity here for couples to feel closer if they mourn the past together and connect emotionally over their anxieties about the future. But some people need to cry and sit with their sadness while others keep busy or devote themselves to new activities to counteract their sad feelings.

When Julia asked Ben if he'd explained to his wife why the kids' departure was affecting him so intensely, he looked at the floor and mumbled, "Carol wouldn't understand."

Why wouldn't she understand? Julia wondered. The couple had been together for decades. Why was it so hard for them to grieve together? Like some struggling empty-nesters, Ben seemed mildly depressed. He seemed to be pining for the past—for the sheer joy of being a dad—and couldn't imagine any possible fulfillment other than raising a family.

Carol's sharp tone, though, seemed to indicate she'd lost patience with what she considered to be his wallowing. But her resentment didn't shake him out of his malaise. It only made him resent her for not feeling the loss of their children as much as he did.

Emotional misalignment is usually made worse by a couple's history of pent-up resentment. The child-rearing years, rosy in retrospect, are often stressful and difficult, and spouses may blame each other during them for a multitude of offenses, such as working too much, not earning enough money, not helping with chores enough, or spending too much time with friends. When the family includes a child with special needs or challenging behavioral or academic issues, spouses often regularly blame each other for the attendant burdens or struggles. Not infrequently, couples allow the blame to build up unexpressed. It becomes an underlying current in the couple's relationship that they never confront or adequately manage. At the empty-nest transition, that resentment is no longer masked by attending to the children's needs and can be suddenly and painfully revealed.

Even if a couple has stayed together for the kids' sake through a marriage of silent resentment or endless bickering, denigration, and blame, a relationship reckoning often occurs once the children leave. A partner may finally say, "Either my spouse will care more about how I feel—after I've experienced so much emotional neglect and hurt—or I will walk away."

Diverging Interests

Even couples in relationships that seem close can find themselves divided during the empty nest. They discover that, without realizing it, their interests have diverged over the years. Carol was surprised to learn that Ben had no desire to take walks or shop. She couldn't relate to his eagerness to spend hours at the gym or in front of the television. Because they had never made it a priority to spend much of their precious time together, pursuing activities as a couple, they were startled to find they had grown into different people—partners they each barely recognized and weren't sure they liked.

At all points in committed relationships, partners need to negotiate their independence and feelings of dependence on each other. It often comes down to finding a sustainable balance between what we call in our practices Me Time and We Time. Too much Me Time may mean the couple has too few mutual interests and activities. Too much We Time, on the other hand, can stifle the need for individual pursuits and growth and ultimately lead to a stale and stultifying marriage.

Finding the right balance becomes even more pressing when the children leave home and both spouses have more time available. They may approach this happily to pursue hobbies, start new businesses, strike up new friendships, and enroll in new classes after years of making school lunches, checking homework, and standing on soccer field sidelines. But both partners need to choose these new pursuits thoughtfully to be sure they enhance, not detract from, the relationship.

Ben had mentioned he was spending a lot of time at the gym. Because Carol wasn't as interested in physical exercise, his choice effectively excluded her. Carol enjoyed going shopping to blow off steam. Ben experienced shopping as torment. They'd both developed activities that reduced their stress and gave them enjoyment, but they hadn't done it together. There wasn't much We Time.

On the other hand, couples can get on each other's nerves with the increased time together. If Carol insisted on running side by side with Ben on adjacent treadmills every time he went to the gym, he might feel he was losing essential Me Time. If Ben had suggested joining Carol's long-standing book group because he thought reading the same things she did and becoming a bigger part of her social life would bring them closer, Carol might feel he was intruding on what had long been an important activity and relationships that were hers alone. Any new life that Ben and Carol crafted would have to be negotiated carefully so each felt neither abandoned nor infringed on.

In our psychotherapy practices, we often suggest to couples long before they become empty-nesters that they develop interests and pursuits as a couple, separate from those of their children. We recommend date nights, occasional weekends away, couple friends, and other activities that do not include the children. We help clients explore what other meaningful interests they may have separate from child-rearing. Even if there is little time, beginning to focus on each other reminds the couple that raising children is an important part of their lives, but not the only important part. Life can have plenty of meaning in the empty nest, but couples need to put in the efforts to create that meaning.

Lack of Relationship-Building Skills

Our American culture tends to value and support couples when they marry and have children. We know what a typical wedding is supposed to look like and can find plenty of advice about how to make one perfect or unusual but always memorable. We have a multitude of often-conflicting guidelines for how to be good parents at all stages of our children's lives. Those earlier life phases are so well studied that most couples have at least some sense of how they are doing compared to the larger population. But we don't have many societal norms regarding what to do after child-rearing has ended.

Many couples lack the tools to negotiate next steps. Effective communication is the most important one. Spouses who haven't talked about the future or imagined together what the possibilities might be may instead resort to complaining about each other. Or they may become defensive, feeling judged or criticized when they do try to talk about the many challenges at this phase of life. In their session with Julia, Ben had responded with irritation to Carol's outreach and withdrawn further. Carol would likely put up with this kind of behavior for only so long before getting fed up. It would take a great effort to help them communicate better and find ways of reconnecting.

Uncovering years of missed opportunities, layers of resentment, old longings, and feelings of betrayal is extremely challenging for couples who inwardly believe that talking about these issues may be extremely risky to their relationship—or that it won't do any good at all. So many couples avoid these concerns for so many years. For there to be a good chance of success, both spouses need to be willing to feel vulnerable, acknowledge mistakes, and forgive the past. They need to be able to focus on the here and now. Letting go of old hurts and power inequities is especially hard for couples when they haven't been adequately discussed, remorse hasn't been expressed, or trust hasn't been reestablished.

Through individual sessions with the couple, Julia learned that Carol had been angry for years about Ben's late hours, travel, and avoidance of housework but had kept her mouth shut for fear of disrupting the peace in the family. Once the children left, though, she felt a need for justice and struggled to express herself to him in a way that he would hear and understand. She wanted to tell him about her sense of disappointment about their marriage but didn't want to alienate him further by being too negative. "I've missed our relationship for years," she told Julia, "but I thought that's what couples did—focus on the children. Now I want us to have the romance we had years ago. I'm not sure how to get there. I don't know if he still loves me. I don't want to be alone."

To strengthen relationships, partners need to remember to regularly turn toward each other throughout and not take each other for granted. With the hectic pace of our daily lives, that's often difficult.

It was easy for Ben and Carol to get caught up in their childcare and work activities. As with too many couples, they ignored the signs that whatever closeness they once had was fading during the busy years of child-rearing and career ladder climbing. They didn't recognize that all relationships require ongoing effort. Failure to build these skills can lead to a breakdown in the relationship.

Julia was not surprised to learn, during an individual session, that Ben had recently considered having an affair with a divorced woman at work who was also an empty-nester. She really listened to him, he said. It is a truism of couples psychology that, when spouses are unhappy within their relationship, they may seek comfort outside the marriage. This is more likely to happen during stressful transitions such as the empty nest as an attempt to manage difficult feelings, such as grief. Especially when they've already been emotionally distant, spouses don't trust each other enough to let themselves be vulnerable and grieve together. They may be constrained by the belief that if they express all their emotions, they will look weak in their spouse's eyes. That leaves them in a lonely place, managing their powerfully sad feelings by themselves. For Ben, the anticipation of a new relationship was a convenient way to sidestep his fears of Carol's judgments while still gaining the support that he needed at a stressful time. He hadn't pursued the affair, he said; he and the woman had only talked. If he did let this new friendship replace his more important connection with Carol, Julia knew, he would sidestep his marriage altogether.

Now at the empty-nest stage, Ben and Carol would have to squarely face the fact that their marriage up to that point had not been as satisfying as they each had hoped. That would be painful. They would have to commit themselves to viewing the empty nest as an opportunity to renegotiate what they expected from their partner to better meet each other's needs. That would be the challenge that would tell whether they had a future together.

Conflicted Family Priorities

The empty-nest period, signaling a shift away from concentrated time with kids, also coincides with the start of other difficult life transitions.

Even when children leave home, they, like Ben and Carol's twins, still have needs. Couples need to negotiate how they will be in this new iteration of family—and they may not always agree. Couples are also feeling more pressure to save for retirement, hopefully not too far down the road. Many now have parents who are aging and need help, or will likely need help in the future. Disagreements about which family resources to devote to each priority is often a source of debate and strife.

Conflict over how much time to spend with aging parents—often at the expense of an immediate family's needs—is an increasingly common issue in our society. (You'll find more about this in Challenge 9: Caregiving.) Even determining the amount of support to give their soon-to-be-adult children can drive a wedge between spouses. Without alignment of values, not just emotions, couples are likely to struggle over the decisions they must make and the changes they must face during the empty-nest phase.

Ben and Carol had had conflicted family priorities even before they had kids. Ben had traveled frequently as he worked his way up from sales to management. This bothered Carol; she thought they should spend more time together. But she never expressed her feelings because he was so good to her once he came home. Besides, she had a job as a corporate attorney and plenty of friends to keep her busy. Then, within two years of their wedding, Carol became pregnant with the twins, and much of their relationship after that became consumed with working as a child-rearing team. Their family priorities coincided.

They went along that way for years, joined through parenting. But as the girls became more independent in their teen years, Carol felt the need to rebalance their priorities to focus more on their marriage. She'd suggest they go to a movie while the girls were spending a busy afternoon on school projects, but Ben insisted on hanging around the house, just in case they needed his help. She asked him more than once to come with her to visit her parents an hour's drive away, but he always declined. Now the twins had gone off to college and Carol wanted to make rekindling their marriage their highest priority. But Ben wasn't ready for that.

On at least one family priority, Ben and Carol wholeheartedly agreed: They didn't want to disappoint their eighteen-year-old girls by breaking up the family. Even so, it seemed to Julia they had nearly reached a breaking point. While they were concerned that separating would hurt the girls, affect their social connections, and cause severe financial difficulties, one or the other usually threatened to leave whenever they fought. They hadn't had sex for years, and Carol suspected that Ben had cheated on her. Ben swore that their lack of sex wasn't a problem for him. Neither really wanted to divorce. But it was becoming more and more difficult to be together.

Tying It All Together

During the next session, Julia asked Carol to try to talk about how she felt about the girls going away to college and the child-rearing phase of her life coming to an end. Julia encouraged her to be thoughtful and as honest as possible and to try not to worry about how Ben might react. She started cautiously, naming obvious changes like no longer feeling connected to the kids' high school and other parents and frequently finding the house quiet. But as she spoke, she bravely began to comment about feeling older and less attractive, not knowing what the future would hold, and feeling lonely and even frightened. Then she looked down and went silent. Ben and Julia waited. Finally, Julia asked Carol what was going on. She looked up with tears in her eyes, shaking her head no.

Ben had been listening carefully with a look of surprise on his face. When he realized that she was crying and that she was trying not to cry, he spontaneously moved closer to her and put his arm around her. Then she cried harder. When she finally calmed down, Julia asked Ben and Carol to look each other in the eye. They looked at each other for a bit and then Ben began to smile. Then Carol did too. It felt like a moment of recognition. Carol had let herself be vulnerable and had allowed Ben to comfort her. He felt needed by her. For a brief instance, they had found some of their old feelings for each other.

Because Carol had allowed herself to feel vulnerable with Ben, he felt able to share his feelings of grief and fears about the future as well. Carol listened without the usual disdain Julia had witnessed in the first sessions. Ben said he'd felt heard for once and his mood seemed to brighten. Carol was able to show sympathy. She reached out and held his hand.

Ben and Carol still had plenty ahead to discuss and negotiate. Restarting their sex life was one hurdle they'd have to address. But that's for another challenge (see Challenge 7).

How to Address Your Empty-Nest Concerns

If you and your partner are approaching or in the empty nest, try the following suggestions—which have worked for our clients—to improve your marriage as you go through this transition.

To start, you and your partner should fill out the following Check-Up separately and then compare your results. There are no right or wrong answers, only places where you and your partner may have diverging or similar feelings, experiences, or hopes and dreams. All are important to know about. The divergent places are opportunities to share and learn so that you can plan mindfully how you'd like your empty-nest life to be.

EMPTY NEST CHECK-UP

1. My partner and I agree about how to spend our free time together and apart.

   Strongly Disagree   Disagree   Neutral   Agree   Strongly Agree

2. My partner and I agree about how much socializing we plan to do together and apart.

   Strongly Disagree   Disagree   Neutral   Agree   Strongly Agree

3. My partner and I agree about whether we'd like to make new friends.

   Strongly Disagree   Disagree   Neutral   Agree   Strongly Agree

4. My partner and I agree about how much time we'd like to spend with our adult children.

   Strongly Disagree   Disagree   Neutral   Agree   Strongly Agree

5. My partner and I feel the same way about letting go of our children.

   Strongly Disagree   Disagree   Neutral   Agree   Strongly Agree

6. My partner and I feel supported when we express to each other the difficult emotions (such as sadness, loneliness, and relief) we sometimes feel about the empty nest.

   Strongly Disagree   Disagree   Neutral   Agree   Strongly Agree

7. My partner and I talk about how we feel about being empty-nesters.

   Strongly Disagree   Disagree   Neutral   Agree   Strongly Agree

8. My partner and I began discussing the empty nest before it happened.

   Strongly Disagree   Disagree   Neutral   Agree   Strongly Agree

9. My partner and I are both satisfied with the amount of time we spend together.

   Strongly Disagree   Disagree   Neutral   Agree   Strongly Agree

10. My partner and I enjoy doing activities and projects together.

   Strongly Disagree   Disagree   Neutral   Agree   Strongly Agree

11. My partner and I feel close to each other.

   Strongly Disagree   **Disagree**   **Neutral**   **Agree**   **Strongly Agree**

12. My partner and I have discussed our hopes and dreams.

   Strongly Disagree   **Disagree**   **Neutral**   **Agree**   **Strongly Agree**

13. My partner and I discuss our feelings about the challenges in our lives.

   Strongly Disagree   **Disagree**   **Neutral**   **Agree**   **Strongly Agree**

14. My partner and I have talked about or made lists of activities we'd like to do.

   Strongly Disagree   **Disagree**   **Neutral**   **Agree**   **Strongly Agree**

15. My partner and I have regular date nights.

   Strongly Disagree   **Disagree**   **Neutral**   **Agree**   **Strongly Agree**

16. My partner and I have occasional weekends away.

   Strongly Disagree   **Disagree**   **Neutral**   **Agree**   **Strongly Agree**

17. My partner and I spend time with other couples.

   Strongly Disagree   **Disagree**   **Neutral**   **Agree**   **Strongly Agree**

18. My partner and I have begun to pursue new interests together.

   Strongly Disagree   **Disagree**   **Neutral**   **Agree**   **Strongly Agree**

19. My partner and I talk about future plans.

   Strongly Disagree   **Disagree**   **Neutral**   **Agree**   **Strongly Agree**

20. My partner and I make the time and effort to focus on our relationship.

   Strongly Disagree   **Disagree**   **Neutral**   **Agree**   **Strongly Agree**

Reviewing the Empty-Nest Check-Up

After you have completed the empty-nest Check-Up, compare your answers to your partner's.

If you have five or more widely diverging answers (on opposite sides of the "neutral" choice): You probably need to address your empty-nest issues.

If you diverge on numbers 5, 6, 7, 11, and 13: It would be a good idea for you to talk more about your feelings and how the transition is affecting each of you.

If you don't agree on numbers 9, 10, 16, 18, and 19: It may be time to renegotiate how you spend your time together and apart, and to find ways to compromise so that each of you gets your needs met.

If you're far apart on number 20: You may want to take stock together of your time management and dedication to the success of your relationship.

Next Steps

If you want to try to improve your emotional connection through the empty-nest transition and increase your ability to cooperate and negotiate to meet the needs of both of you, here's what we suggest:

The following process may feel slow and labored, but it's likely that you haven't felt emotionally close for a while. Try to be patient; this will give you the best opportunity to fully know what your partner is thinking and feeling, and your partner will learn what you are thinking and feeling. This is an opportunity to get to know each other deeply during this major life transition. If you both agree to take your time with it, you will get the most from it.

Both of you should first review the "Tips for Talking and Listening" found at the beginning of this book. Read through the guidelines until you feel familiar with them. Then find a time to sit down together and share your Check-Up responses, focusing on the similarities and differences. Listen carefully to learn how your partner is feeling about the empty-nest transition. Don't make any decisions at this time; just practice talking and listening according to the guidelines. Make an effort to reserve judgment and to support each other.

A Week Later

Of course, one conversation isn't enough to substantially change a decades-long relationship. Sharing your feelings, frustrations, hopes, and fears about the future will help you feel that you are making a joint effort to be emotionally closer. You are building meaning into your relationship and your lives together and your time apart.

About a week after you discuss your Check-Up results, meet again to share any additional reactions to your findings and begin formulating a plan to improve your relationship.

Here are some questions to spur your conversation:

- Do you need to make time specifically for sharing your feelings about the children leaving?
- Do you need to talk about old hurts or feelings of betrayal so that you can acknowledge them and move on?
- Do you need to plan activities together that you might both enjoy?
- Do you need to build a social circle together by spending time with other couples or in group activities?
- What do each of you hope for going forward?

- Are there ways that you can help each other achieve your goals and build more meaning into your lives?
- What do each of you want and need?
- Do you each want more time together? More time pursuing separate activities? Can you negotiate your time in a thoughtful, caring, cooperative way so that you both feel satisfied?

Make a plan to regularly schedule two types of activities: time together engaged in something you both value, and time apart to pursue your individual interests. Commit to sharing your feelings about both kinds of activities. Reflect on how each of you feels about doing things together and separately. Find a compromise, if necessary, to meet the needs of both of you.

An Ongoing Plan to Integrate Change

We've found that lasting change doesn't really take hold unless you also spend time reviewing and fine-tuning the plan you've created. Schedule a regular meeting, not just to be together but to reflect on how your relationship is going. Some of our clients have felt uncomfortable doing this at first, but when they get past any awkwardness, they soon find that they look forward to nurturing their relationship in this way. The reliable time evolves into an opportunity to connect to each other.

Sharing your feelings, even the difficult ones, brings you closer, increases your knowledge of each other, and leads to a greater sense of trust. Even when you are frustrated, using the "Tips for Talking and Listening" can help you work through your issues to get to an increased level of mutual understanding and closeness. Sometimes the most difficult conversations lead to the greatest sense of satisfaction.

Talk about how you are each feeling about what you have learned about each other and how you both feel about the time spent together and apart. You don't have to agree, but you should be accepting and respectful as you continue to work on your changing relationship. Your goal is to feel more connected. Even if you continue to work on areas in which you disagree, try to share feelings, remember shared experiences, grieve together, and aim for compromise and good boundaries.

Steps to Success

Couples have plenty of work to do to make the empty-nest transition as successful as possible. Keep the following steps in mind as you go.

- Strengthen your emotional bond through sharing feelings and setting aside times to talk about those difficult feelings, past and present.
- Listen without judgment.
- Plan activities together and pursue new experiences.
- Negotiate time together and apart.
- Align priorities around family.
- Have conversations about the future.

The empty nest is an opportunity for both of you to grow together and separately. Exploring new interests and pursuits and increasing your feelings of connection will create meaning in this new and exciting phase of your life together.

Challenge 2

Extended Family

"Mom, it's Hope." Elaine's daughter's voice sounded almost frantic on the phone. "I know it's a lot to ask, but I have nowhere else to go. Can we stay with you and Phil for a while until I get back on my feet?" Without waiting for her mother's reply, Hope went on quickly, "The kids are having such a tough time, Mom. Money is tight. I'm overwhelmed and could really use some help."

Elaine loved her daughter and her three young grandchildren. She had known Hope's divorce would be emotionally messy and financially devastating, and she'd been half-expecting this call. In that instant, all she wanted to do was rescue them. "Yes. Of course," Elaine responded immediately. "You know we're here for you. Stay as long as you need."

Later that night, when Elaine announced to Phil that Hope and her children would be moving in with them soon, he became alarmed. He'd never tell Elaine, although he'd talked with Julia about it in an individual therapy session in the past, but since Hope was six—when he came into her life and her biological father had disappeared after Elaine's divorce from him—Phil's feelings toward her as a stepfather had been complicated and more critical than those a father might have had. He had always found her to be a handful. He wasn't surprised that, at age thirty-eight, she still wasn't able to stand fully on her own two feet.

He did love Hope and the grandchildren and knew the four-bedroom house that he and Elaine owned could accommodate them. He wasn't sure, though, that he could tolerate having them underfoot. His peaceful mornings drinking coffee in the kitchen with the sun streaming in would be replaced by chaos. He didn't want Hope to think she could just move in permanently. *She needs to stay independent,* he thought. But he could never share those concerns with Elaine without infuriating her and threatening their marriage.

The sudden intrusion of any family members can disrupt the lives of even long-contented couples. Whether faced with requests for free shelter, babysitting, or financial help, spouses must jointly decide the right ways to respond. If they don't agree about the importance of family loyalty, desires for providing care and pleasing others, and the need to establish limits, then they will have simmering resentment and recurring arguments.

Elaine and Phil, like so many couples over fifty since the 2008 Great Recession, suddenly faced a strenuous test for successfully balancing contrasting needs: adult children returning to the nest, dubbed "boomerang children." Their returns are usually prompted by economic circumstances, such as unemployment, poor job prospects, chronic underachievement, and large amounts of student loan debt, but are also associated with other factors, including lack of college completion, mental or physical disability, chronic illness, and just plain rotten luck. Even as the US economy has recovered, boomerang children haven't disappeared.

Parents often feel obliged or eager to provide the needed support. But then the couple's plans for their future retirement, financial management, and downsizing can be sidetracked, if not completely derailed. In fact, a study of baby boomers indicated that supporting adult children can determine when and if spouses retire: Only 21 percent of baby boomers who still support adult children are retired, compared with 52 percent of boomer households whose adult children are financially independent.

Spouses can quickly become frustrated with the kids and each other. For those who struggle with the needs of extended-family members, including caring for aging parents (see Challenge 9), four main reasons often arise: diverging values, conflicted family priorities, inadequate communication and planning, and a lack of team building.

Diverging Values

When couples disagree about how much to support their adult children (regardless of whether those children have returned home), they struggle to reach a compromise that feels fair and satisfactory to both spouses. These disagreements are often rife with emotion and blame. One spouse believes the other to be enabling the adult child's dependence rather than encouraging her independence. The other spouse sees the first as heartless and stingy, selfishly depriving and neglecting the needs of the child. Cooperation between the spouses breaks down. The frustration that results tests their loyalties to their children and each other, straining their marital relationship, sometimes to the breaking point.

Elaine and Phil's situation was not unusual. Hope was in crisis and needed emotional and financial support. Should Elaine's determination to help her daughter overrule Phil's opinion that Hope needed to be self-sufficient, or vice versa? If Phil agreed to allow Hope and the grandchildren to move into their home, then would they stay indefinitely? Or for a limited time—say, six months? No guidebook can prescribe the right amounts and types of help. These are all value-based questions with no absolute right or wrong answers. If Elaine and Phil could negotiate cooperatively, then they'd be more likely to manage the situation effectively and strengthen, not weaken, their marriage.

Like most couples, however, Elaine and Phil hadn't sat down together to hatch a plan for any of this. Elaine had spontaneously, unilaterally, said yes to Hope. Spouses often assume they agree about these kinds of family issues far more than they do. There can be complicating factors. Cultural differences within the couple can expose conflicting values. One spouse may find it consistent with what she believes and what her parents taught her to continue to care for adult children, while the other spouse may feel it's best for adult children to find a way to stand on their own two feet because that was what he learned growing up. There's a lot at stake here. Spouses may tolerate a partner's stinging criticism but will forcefully reject negative judgments about the values that were taught by their respective parents and cultural communities. They may become defensive, digging in their heels to do battle.

These tensions are heightened in a "blended family"—when a couple has children from previous relationships. Back when Elaine and Phil were growing up in the 1950s, most families in the United States looked fairly typical: two married parents—the man a breadwinner, the woman a housewife—and two or so children. Nowadays, the picture is strikingly different. Some 80 percent of children live in families that don't resemble that picture much at all. With the 50 percent increase in divorce among baby boomers over the past twenty years, families with stepsiblings and half siblings have become commonplace. According to a 2015 Pew Research Center report on the American family, 16 percent of children today (about one in six) are part of a blended family. Often, the households have been joined but the values of stepfamily members haven't blended. As in the case of Elaine and Phil, when one spouse's child is asking for help, the birth parent frequently bridles at any perceived criticism of her child-rearing decisions. It can be easy for her current spouse to blame her, her ex-spouse, and the child herself for her lack of initiative and accomplishment, and as a result, he may feel little sympathy or responsibility for the child's plight. Or he may feel he has no authority as a stepparent and is helpless to assist the child. These issues frequently come up when the children are young but also arise when they are older. The unresolved differences of opinions between the spouses can be a never-ending source of disgruntlement that crests when the adult child makes a humble and unplanned request—for shelter, money, or other support. Many factors can come into play here, such as the child's circumstances, the history of relationships in the blended family, and the family's cultural backgrounds. What's common across the board, though, is that the birth parents and stepparents need to communicate to align their values as much as possible.

Conflicted Family Priorities

A second reason for difficulties can be conflicting priorities, which can result from each spouse's personal histories. That was the case with Elaine and Phil. As Julia had learned in past couples sessions, Elaine's parents weren't supportive when she was going through her own divorce, telling her dismissively to "Go back to your husband." Ever since Hope was young, Elaine swore to herself that if her daughter were ever in a similar situation, she wouldn't abandon her like her own parents did. Despite her love for Phil, supporting her daughter in need always outweighed all other concerns.

Phil, on the other hand, had had to fend for himself since he was eighteen because his parents could no longer afford to support him.

He felt he'd been lucky to have to learn to be self-reliant and believed that other young people deserved the same chance. His priorities at this point in life were different from Elaine's. He didn't want to lean on anybody or have anybody lean on him; he just wanted to enjoy more time with his wife. He and she were not on the same page.

Conflict in these types of situations occurs not only when one spouse is more eager than the other to help an adult child. One may want to live close to grandchildren, while the other is eager to move to a warmer climate. One may insist on providing a loan for an adult child's first home or graduate school, while the other blanches at the cost. And one may want to have Sunday night dinner every week with the extended clan, while the other would limit contact to holiday dinners three times a year. If their priorities diverge dramatically, couples will always have underlying or overt tension.

Just as with values, aligning priorities is more difficult for blended families like Phil and Elaine's. As psychologist and stepfamily expert Patricia Papernow has pointed out, blended-family dynamics don't occur only in families with young children but also with adult children, and in those older families, parents and stepparents can differ sharply in their expectations for the adult children. "Stepparents want stepchildren to 'be independent,'" she said. "What is 'good parenting' to the parent may be seen as 'enabling' to the stepparent." This can lead to conflicting family priorities as time goes by.

Papernow has also observed that in stepfamilies, children experience "loyalty binds" in which they feel caught between being loyal toward one biological parent or another or between a biological parent and a stepparent. Phil had certainly seen this with Hope over the years. Like many children with stepparents, she had at times been aloof and at other times clingy. He was never quite sure whether she needed him to act as a supportive friend or a parental authority figure. Then when she was in a rebellious teenage period, she was highly disrespectful toward him. He had understood that that's what adolescents do but was still left with some lingering feelings of wariness toward her. Frankly, he'd been relieved when she finally moved out.

Parents and stepparents struggle with issues of loyalty as well. They may feel ambivalent and unsure of how to proceed, racked with guilt no matter what choice they make. A biological mother may fear what may happen if she doesn't support her adult child or if she sets limits on that support. Would that daughter become distraught? So distraught as to turn her back on her mother? Would the daughter not only feel hurt but also blame her biological parent and stepparent for her own problems?

But consider the opposite scenario in which the biological parent is loyal to her child first and her spouse second. The marital relationship surely suffers, at least to a degree. The stepparent may feel disrespected, ignored, and frustrated that he has no say in the management of the situation with the adult child. He may feel sidelined and become angry with both his spouse and the adult child for causing a rift in their marriage.

Grandchildren can become another source of conflicting priorities. Many partners over fifty are eager to become grandparents and overjoyed when that grandchild finally arrives. They want to spend as much time with their children's growing family as their children will allow. For them, babysitting is a treat, not a chore, and buying gifts, baking cookies, and pushing the stroller to the park are the stuff dreams are made of. But when one spouse is more connected to the children and grandchildren than the other—or when one prioritizes time with the grandchildren and the other chooses not to—they will be at odds. They both can justify their perspective and argue that their interests should take precedence. And each may feel criticized and misunderstood by the other.

This became true for Elaine and Phil. Within a week of receiving that first call, Elaine had arranged two bedrooms, one of which had been Phil's office. They looked like something at a bed-and-breakfast, with pretty bedspreads and matching curtains, filled with lots of new toys. Phil wasn't delighted about the unnecessary cost, but he kept his mouth shut. When Hope and the children arrived, she hugged Phil and started to cry. Elaine beamed. She'd made a special dinner with chocolate pudding for dessert. Phil could hardly eat.

When couples who are faced with conflicting family priorities come to see us for help working out their differences, we encourage them to each put themselves in their partner's position and imagine what he or she is feeling. An important first step in approaching a better alignment as a couple is to increase awareness of the forces from the past, the wishes and needs that each partner is managing, and how these play a role in their decisions and choices. As each spouse begins to more deeply understand the perspective of the other, they can then more empathically work toward reaching compromises both can live with.

Inadequate Communication and Planning

No disagreement between partners about adult children is easily resolved without communication as early and often as possible. But couples frequently neglect to reflect together on the nature and extent of assistance to their extended-family members that they could or should provide. "Whatever it takes"—which is basically what Elaine said in response to Hope's request—is not always the best answer, especially if spouses haven't talked through the implications of the commitments they are willing to make. They need to sit down to consider together how devoting time to a family member's needs will affect them as individuals and as a couple. If it's a financial request, they need to assess what they can realistically afford given their current and retirement needs.

Mostly, though, they need to negotiate and compromise. No matter how committed a couple may be to the well-being of their extended family, they must work together to set some limits on the time and resources expended. They need to agree to protect some time that is just for them—time they will not allow to be interrupted by the needs of others. If extended family moves in, the couple may need protected space as well—for instance, a bedroom or office—that is strictly off-limits to the extended-family members. A set of household rules should also be discussed. Of course, partners then need to stand shoulder to shoulder to enforce those rules. And spouses need to be aligned when it comes to assisting extended family financially. Consider the amount and terms, and consequences if the terms aren't met. Without discussing these issues—repeatedly—the marriage may flounder.

After Hope moved in, months went by, with Phil feeling increasingly frustrated but not sharing his feelings with Elaine, who spent so much time with Hope and the kids that she seemed to forget about him. The budget that he and Elaine had planned out carefully was tossed aside as she cared for the additional family of four. Hope took over the formal living room, filling it with her belongings and talking loudly on her cell phone at all hours, even when Phil tried to watch television in the next room. Elaine didn't seem to be aware of his discomfort, and he said nothing.

As with many spouses in this situation, money worries gnawed continually at Phil. He resented that Elaine was on a spending spree for Hope and the grandchildren, drawing on marital savings without conferring with him. But as with many other parents, Elaine's identity was wrapped up in being a good mom above all else, even to her own possible financial and marital detriment. Their respective views were deeply held with strong emotion. Little wonder that spouses in this predicament can begin to feel they aren't understood. Their empathy for each other may steadily diminish as their anger slowly increases. It may escalate to the point where they can no longer talk about their child without instantly fighting.

In a situation such as Elaine and Phil's, the sooner they can sit down together to talk through their needs and wishes regarding extended family, the better. Most partners are aware of their differing perspectives but avoid discussing them because they don't want to have an all-out fight. Yet talking it through allows the couple to develop a compromise plan that meets some of each of their needs and gives both a sense of what the future may hold. This allows the couple to manage the addition to their household or the additional expense together, actually reducing the ultimate likelihood of a disagreement.

Lack of Team Building

On the afternoon that Phil received a phone call from his doctor, their home situation reached a crisis. He was anxious about some physical symptoms he'd been having and eager to get the results of his latest blood test. The noise level was so high in the living room that even when he went into the next room, he couldn't hear what the doctor was saying. No one seemed to notice that he was on the phone. Suddenly, Phil was yelling. "Shut up! Can't you see I'm on the phone? I can't take it anymore!" There was silence.

Phil received his reassuring test results, went straight to the bedroom, and slammed the door. He felt embarrassed about losing control. But he also felt angry that the life he'd worked so hard for had been taken away. He didn't come out for dinner that night and went to bed without talking to anyone.

In the morning before the kids were up, Phil asked Elaine to take a walk with him. She agreed, and they left the house and headed out into the neighborhood. Phil put his arm around her, kissed her cheek, and said, "We need to make a plan."

Elaine immediately bristled. "I can't kick Hope and the kids out," she said. "They're having a hard time. How could you be so selfish?"

He said gently, "I would never prevent you from being there for your family, and I know you wouldn't do that to me either." He took a big breath. "But we need to talk about how to make this work for all of us. Maybe we should make an appointment to talk to Julia."

Elaine was quiet for a moment. She didn't want Phil to be unhappy, but she also couldn't let Hope down. She'd gotten so caught up in caring for Hope and the kids that she'd pushed Phil to the back burner. Maybe off the burner altogether. She knew he was right. She agreed to a session with Julia.

Ideally, couples have conversations long before damage is done to the relationship. But even if couples have argued and hurt each other's feelings, talking together is still the only way to make repairs. While some studies have found that the return of an adult child may be beneficial to a couple's relationship, it can happen only if the partners forge a sense of teamwork. Team members may not agree on every issue, but they have committed themselves to working together as a unit. Teams have common goals and strategies. They huddle regularly to discuss developments and plans. They make adjustments together as needed. For a team of spouses helping an adult child, that means pursuing the same mission (caring for the younger generations and themselves as well) and the same means (shifting time and resources, setting limits, and nurturing all family relationships).

The adult children and even grandchildren have to be on the team, too. Sometimes, the boundaries between the adult child and the couple may become blurred and the adult child is permitted to make decisions that should be made by the couple. Sometimes none of the adults plays a disciplinary role, allowing the grandchildren to have the run of the house. All parties need to talk during scheduled family meetings about getting on the same page. All need to play a role in the process so that even prolonged visits to the couple's home by extended-family members don't compromise anyone's quality of life.

Tying It All Together

On their walk back to the house, Phil suggested that he and Elaine come up with some basic house rules, financial limits, and a plan to have some time alone together. Then he paused, knowing what he had to say next would be hard for Elaine to hear. He suggested they come up with a timeline for Hope that included a plan to help her and the children move out. They'd make an appointment to talk it through with Julia.

Elaine winced slightly but thought about what Phil had proposed. She always knew that this arrangement would have to come to an end one day—as much for the sake of her child and grandchildren as for her and her husband. She told Phil she'd be willing to see what they could come up with while still supporting Hope. They agreed to schedule a couples therapy session and then to have lunch afterward at a local diner, just the two of them, and work on the details of this plan. Once they had worked out their own differences in expectations and preferences and arrived at an acceptable compromise, they would sit down with Hope to talk with her about it and learn her perspective.

As they headed back to the house, Elaine reached out and held Phil's hand. They opened the front door to the chatter of three young children having breakfast. They both smiled. They would find a way to work it out.

By early the following week, they'd met with Julia to clarify what they'd both be comfortable saying to Hope. They wanted to present a plan that took everyone's needs into account. They practiced with Julia until both felt that they were ready to address Hope together. As Julia explained, "Try to think of it this way: You have invited Hope and her children into your home so that she can more easily get back on her feet. That's the positive goal. You all want that to happen. You are putting limits around it that should be beneficial to all of you. But most importantly, you need to support each other first, and then you can support her as a team."

When they finally sat down with Hope to let her know that they'd been talking about a plan and wanted to bring her in on it, she was relieved. As she put it, "I've been feeling awkward because I don't want to be a burden and I know it's stressful having us underfoot." Together, Phil and Elaine brought up some issues that would make her stay with them more comfortable, such as keeping the noise level down, budgeting expenses, and increasing privacy. They also asked her to talk about a time frame. Despite expressing her anxiety about the future, she agreed to a tentative date to move out. They all agreed that they'd talk again soon about how things were going and what each of them needed along the way.

How to Address Your Extended-Family Concerns

If you and your partner are having issues with your extended family, consider taking the following Check-Up.

You and your partner should fill out the Check-Up separately and then compare your results. There are no right or wrong answers, only places where you and your partner may have diverging or similar feelings, experiences, or needs. All are important to know about. The divergent places are opportunities to share and learn so that you can plan mindfully how you'd like to improve your relationship with regard to your extended family.

EXTENDED FAMILY CHECK-UP

1. My partner and I approach our family as a team.

   Strongly Disagree   Disagree   Neutral   Agree   Strongly Agree

2. My partner and I agree on the amount of time to spend with family.

   Strongly Disagree   Disagree   Neutral   Agree   Strongly Agree

3. My partner and I are both eager to help out family when they are in need.

   Strongly Disagree   Disagree   Neutral   Agree   Strongly Agree

4. My partner and I give each other freedom to have separate relationships with family.

   Strongly Disagree   Disagree   Neutral   Agree   Strongly Agree

5. My partner and I agree about how much financial help to provide family.

   Strongly Disagree   Disagree   Neutral   Agree   Strongly Agree

6. My partner and I agree about how much childcare or eldercare we should provide.

   Strongly Disagree   Disagree   Neutral   Agree   Strongly Agree

7. My partner and I agree about whether to allow family to live with us.

   Strongly Disagree   Disagree   Neutral   Agree   Strongly Agree

8. My partner and I have discussed how we feel about family living in our home.

   Strongly Disagree   Disagree   Neutral   Agree   Strongly Agree

9. My partner and I respectfully listen to each other's views about family.

   Strongly Disagree   Disagree   Neutral   Agree   Strongly Agree

10. My partner and I compromise when it comes to decisions about family.

    Strongly Disagree   Disagree   Neutral   Agree   Strongly Agree

11. My partner and I are supportive of each other's views about family even when we disagree.

Strongly Disagree   Disagree   Neutral   Agree   Strongly Agree

12. My partner and I don't allow problems with family members to come between us.

Strongly Disagree   Disagree   Neutral   Agree   Strongly Agree

13. My partner and I accept that we have different relationships with family members.

Strongly Disagree   Disagree   Neutral   Agree   Strongly Agree

14. My partner and I take a long view of family relationships, knowing that things change over time.

Strongly Disagree   Disagree   Neutral   Agree   Strongly Agree

15. My partner and I agree on a balance of family time and socializing with friends.

Strongly Disagree   Disagree   Neutral   Agree   Strongly Agree

16. My partner and I peaceably agree to disagree about some family issues.

Strongly Disagree   Disagree   Neutral   Agree   Strongly Agree

17. My partner and I try to enjoy family when we can.

Strongly Disagree   Disagree   Neutral   Agree   Strongly Agree

18. My partner and I put each other first, before other family members.

Strongly Disagree   Disagree   Neutral   Agree   Strongly Agree

19. My partner and I are realistic about how complicated family relationships can be.

Strongly Disagree   Disagree   Neutral   Agree   Strongly Agree

20. My partner and I try hard to create a comfortable family situation for both of us.

Strongly Disagree   Disagree   Neutral   Agree   Strongly Agree

Reviewing the Extended-Family Check-Up

If you differ by two or more degrees on 1, 2, 3, 5, or 6: Take some time to discuss extended-family concerns including finances, time together, and childcare. Use the following guidelines to ask questions and listen to the answers to better understand each other's values.

If you differ on 4, 13, or 15: Have a focused conversation about how much space you need when it comes to family, and how much time together and apart you'd like to spend with family.

If you differ on 16, 17, 19, or 20: Discuss the tension that you experience regarding family issues and how to decrease it.

If you differ on 9, 10, 11, 12, or 18: Talk about how you can support each other better as you address issues with extended families.

Next Steps

Our suggestions for facing the challenges posed by extended-family members' needs use the same framework as described in the previous challenge: We recommend a long and intensive listening session. After enough time has elapsed for you to thoughtfully and unemotionally ponder the first conversation's exchange, follow it with a concerted problem-solving session.

To find consensus and reach viable solutions, you'll first need to sufficiently listen and develop increased empathy for your partner. The following listening process may feel slow and labored, and coming to a compromised, cooperative place will likely take a while. Try to be patient; this will give you the best opportunity to fully know what your partner is thinking and feeling, and your partner will learn what you are thinking and feeling. This is an opportunity to get to know each other deeply regarding this major life challenge. If you both agree to take your time with it, then you will get the most from it.

Make an appointment with each other to sit down together for an hour. You won't be making big decisions; you'll be sharing your Check-Up results and talking about where you agree and disagree. Take turns telling each other how you feel about your relationship with your extended family. Use the "Tips for Talking and Listening" found at the beginning of this book.

Remember that your goal is to feel more connected. End the hour by identifying areas of agreement from the Check-Up and setting a positive goal, such as planning an outing or finding a project you can work on together. This will be an opportunity to feel closer.

A Week Later

Because your feelings and beliefs about extended family have developed over years, you'll need more time to review the Check-Up and discuss areas of agreement and disagreement. The goal is to work toward a mutually acceptable compromise in which both of you feel heard and supported.

About a week after you discuss your Check-Up results, meet again to share any additional reactions to your findings and begin formulating a plan to improve your relationship with regard to your extended family.

Here are some questions—which you can tailor to your particular situation—to spur your conversation:

- What are your expectations for how independent and self-sufficient your adult children should be?
- What does this mean for you financially now and in the future?
- How much time do you want to dedicate to extended family?
- What roles do you see adult children and grandchildren playing in your lives now?
- What roles do you want to play in their lives?

- What kind of balance among individual, couple, and family priorities do you each attempt to maintain for yourselves?
- What do each of you hope for going forward?
- Are there ways that you can help each other achieve your goals?
- What do each of you want and need from each other?
- How can you negotiate your needs in a thoughtful, caring, cooperative way so that you both feel satisfied?

Each of you should consider how willing you are to compromise when it comes to each issue that arises. Remember that you are trying to take care of yourself and each other through this process. You both will have to compromise. Take your partner's perspectives into account as you negotiate changes. Nothing will be written in stone. It is likely that you will need to revisit many extended-family issues repeatedly as time goes by and circumstances change. Even if you can't reach agreement on everything, having the conversations, expressing your feelings and opinions, and listening to each other will bring you closer.

An Ongoing Plan to Integrate Change

All plans need regular review and refinement to remain fresh, relevant, and effective. Meet again at least monthly to talk about how you are both feeling, what you need, and how you might assist each other. As you continue to negotiate compromise, keep in mind the implications of the decisions you are making. What personal sacrifices can you tolerate making? The more concrete and detailed you can be in your conversations, the less likely you are to encounter misunderstanding and disagreement later.

Share your reflections about the ongoing extended-and-blended family challenges. You won't likely agree in full, but you should be accepting and respectful as you continue to search for workable compromises. Your goal is to nurture your relationship by demonstrating your care for each other as you face challenges and adversity together. Even as you continue to work on areas in which you disagree, try to share feelings, remember shared experiences, discuss your family values, and aim for good boundaries.

Steps to Success

Extended families can be tough for couples to manage successfully. Step up to the challenge together for the best chance of making the most of your unique, complex family:

- Make an effort to thoroughly understand your partner's perspective on extended family, both in relation to the past and currently.
- Acknowledge each other's sense of responsibility and loyalty to the family member in need.
- Communicate about your feelings frequently and respond supportively.
- Approach the issues that arise in the family as a team.
- Spend time together to thoughtfully hammer out a compromise that takes the needs and wishes of both of you into account.
- Consult a professional if you struggle to make a plan that is mutually acceptable.

The critical premise is that the couple's relationship is of primary importance. Relationships with extended family follow from there. You and your partner should take care of each other first before making a plan to care for a family member. Then together, you will be better able to join forces to judiciously and realistically support each other while you make efforts to help others.

Challenge 3

Finances

James and Grace rushed past Barry into his office and immediately sat in their usual spots on his couch: as far from each other as possible, hugging opposite arms. They'd been meeting with Barry for brief courses of couples therapy for several years—whenever their arguing escalated to the point that one or the other couldn't take it anymore. Between counseling sessions, they relied on their large extended family and many friends from their close-knit African American church to help them referee what seemed like constant disagreements.

Through thirty-five years of marriage, they had struggled together through the deaths of close family members, financial problems, and a house fire. Their three adult children—their two daughters and Grace's son from a previous marriage—had troubles that weighed heavily on the couple. They tended to take out their frustrations on each other and often seemed exasperated with each other. But Barry knew that James and Grace, both nearing sixty, were still dedicated to the conviction that marriage and family were lifetime commitments. So they soldiered on, bickering all the while.

Before Barry could even shut his office door, James began: "When I saw the delivery truck pull up, I turned to Grace, who was watching one of those TV shows, and I said, 'What's this?' Of course, I knew what it was." Barry knew, too. He'd been through this with them before. Grace had ordered something—actually, some things—from the shopping network. James turned toward Grace on the couch and said, his voice raised not quite to a yell: "How many times do we have to talk about this? We don't have the money. You can't keep ordering things!"

"I've tried to explain to him many times that the lotion they sell, the one with the lily scent, works for my skin," Grace said. "It was only three payments of $12.99, and they threw in body wash!" She leaned toward Barry and continued, "Why does he have to pitch a fit every time? How else am I supposed to get my lotion?"

For many couples, bickering over finances can seem as common as nagging about who takes out the trash. In fact, finances are the leading cause of marital stress, studies show. But for couples over fifty, the financial stressors can add up: saving for retirement or retiring, paying for kids' college and weddings, managing accumulated debt, covering medical bills, and caregiving expenses.

Beyond these big-ticket items, certain issues and questions come up frequently: How much are we spending on haircuts or, in Grace's case, lotion? How often should we eat out? Can we afford a vacation? Buy new clothes? Help extended-family members in need? Go to a coffee shop or even the theater with a friend?

Trying to sort out which needs are most important, especially when funds are limited and values and priorities differ, heightens the tension. One spouse may feel more comfortable spending to enjoy life, assuming they'll have enough, while the other may lean toward frugality to ensure they don't outlive their savings. This difference in their views can cause both spouses to feel that their needs are not being met. Either spouse—or both—may cast blame overtly or covertly. Many couples don't like to talk about finances for fear of causing conflict. So they sidestep the subject entirely. As they get older, even couples who are comfortable financially often need to reevaluate priorities and shift resources to plan together for their future. Couples with a reduced income may need to tighten their belts. Whatever their financial situation, couples often don't discuss and prepare themselves for changes. Financial struggles can challenge even the most compatible couples. And when they do, tension rises.

You will likely live longer than your parents and your grandparents—possibly decades more—and you will need more money than they did. There are calculators to predict, however imperfectly, approximately how long you will live and how much money you will need. (See AARP's calculators at www.aarp.org/retirementcalculator.) Other calculators can help you predict, based on your earnings and savings, your projected income in retirement.

Over our years in practice, we have learned that there is usually no simple fix for couples' disagreements about money. James and Grace were no exception. We have discovered, too, that the way couples feel about money and manage their finances often reflects underlying emotional issues as well as their interpersonal dynamics.

But we have seen clients change those patterns and transform their relationships around money. You can too. This challenge helps you uncover the reasons for your financial struggles and learn to take the reins together to responsibly manage your financial lives. All couples have a stake in being financially informed and managing their economic future together. We'll start by looking at stumbling blocks to financial equanimity—feeling an imbalance of power, disagreeing about needs versus emotional spending, and having difficulty compromising—and then help you find solutions in financial teamwork.

Imbalance of Power

At any marital phase, an imbalance of power regarding finances can indicate long-standing control and trust issues. The controlling spouse may have grown up with economic instability and now feels secure only when he has the last word on what happens with their money. Or an imbalance may have developed over years when a partner believes the other lacks financial competence and responsibility. It's also possible that one spouse wants to be cared for by the other, stating, "I'm just not good with money." This arrangement may work well for many years but can begin to cause problems once older couples experience financial or health problems—they now both need to know how to pay the bills, prioritize spending, and know where the keys to the safe-deposit box are. With changed circumstances, some couples can renegotiate control; others resist and often have more conflict.

This was the case for Grace and James. Grace bristled at James's bossiness over control of their money. It incensed her that he would sometimes go to the sporting goods store and buy a new fishing pole or hunting knife—after forcing her to return her lotions. He may have felt entitled to treating himself, but what about what she wanted? He never even asked.

It hadn't always been that way. For many years, James had ceded control over the money to Grace because he didn't want to have to think about it. She handled the finances well, but she also had the freedom to buy lotion when she wanted it. After she had several small strokes a year earlier, however, he had taken over their finances completely because she'd forgotten to pay a few bills. Grace admitted that she'd experienced some confusion after the strokes but felt she'd recovered well enough to continue to handle the finances. James disagreed and also argued that she had trouble signing checks now; the strokes had left her with some numbness in her fingers.

As his own anxieties escalated because of their economic precariousness, James took the reins more forcefully. Unable to confront him directly and resolve the power struggle, Grace resorted to spending behind his back and, when he found out, arguing with him over it. As their financial pressure mounted, she thought he was reacting by becoming both more controlling and more capricious in his dictatorial decision-making. Grace resented it more and more.

In our psychotherapy practices, we often help couples negotiate around one partner's controlling behavior by examining why he feels the need to control his spouse. What would happen if he stopped? Often there is either an underlying fear of his own loss of control, or a fear that his partner will take control or use bad judgment and he won't be able to rein her in. Sometimes these fears stem from old traumatic experiences that led to feelings of vulnerability and helplessness and have little to do with the other partner, and sometimes the controlling behavior accurately reflects the other partner's tendency to spend impulsively.

As James and Grace complained, Barry was aware that their bickering over small purchases was likely the tip of the iceberg of their concerns about their finances and their future. Many older couples fear that they will outlive their money and worry about what they would do then. He knew that if Grace and James shared their financial concerns, they were more likely to be able to renegotiate a better balance of power when it came to their money.

With Barry's encouragement, Grace and James admitted that they both felt increasingly anxious about their reduced income and scant savings. They had grown up in working-class families and had then worked hard all their lives to achieve solid middle-middle-class status. James owned a small electronics store, and Grace had been an office manager. She'd stopped working after the strokes, although she'd recovered pretty well, except for the numbness in her fingers that made it difficult to type and write. Without her income, they were afraid they could easily slip down a rung or two on the socioeconomic ladder. Would they be able to afford Grace's ongoing medical bills? What if they needed a new roof or car or couldn't pay their property taxes? What if James developed a health problem and could no longer work? And if he lost his business, what would they do then? At this point, James worried that he'd never be able to retire. Grace had no employer retirement benefit; her jobs had always been part-time without benefits. Fortunately, James would get a small pension from a previous employer, but they worried that that plus Social Security benefits wouldn't cover their needs, much less their wants.

Over the next sessions, Barry helped James and Grace see that they weren't addressing their financial concerns as a team but were instead each clambering for control, each feeling that he or she knew best. The battle over control made their ability to manage their worries even harder. They weren't supporting each other, solving problems together, or making a plan for the future that they could both live with. Instead they were fighting over lotion. That made no sense. But it wasn't surprising.

Needs Versus Emotional Spending

Many couples over fifty share James and Grace's anxieties because of economic downturns, layoffs, and other unexpected setbacks. There is good reason for that. According to a 2016 Gallup poll of middle-aged Americans' attitudes, 59 percent are concerned about not saving enough money for retirement, 53 percent about paying for medical bills in the event of an emergency, and 35 percent about being unable to afford their children's college costs. Those worries are likely warranted. Nearly half of households headed by someone fifty-five or older have no retirement savings or pension benefits. Of those families who have saved money, the mean amount is about $95,000—not enough for the years and needs ahead. More than 30 percent of Americans over age sixty-five are economically insecure, according to the Kaiser Family Foundation. They may have increasing healthcare costs (including medications, co-pays, and insurance premiums), mortgage debt, and adult children and grandchildren who need support. This is just one of the reasons that more Americans are working after age sixty-five than at any time since the turn of the century. And it is little wonder that battling over the finances is the greatest cause of strife for so many couples. Fear and scarcity often lead to belt-tightening. But for it to be effective, partners need to work together to define what they need versus what they can live without.

Sometimes the financial struggles that couples have aren't about needs. Some find themselves arguing over what the priorities are when it comes to spending beyond what's required. "The root of this discord," reports one survey, "is differing opinion on what constitutes spending on 'needs' versus 'wants.'" This conflict often becomes more pointed for partners over fifty, who can face tougher financial challenges. Basic needs are usually clear to both partners, but beyond that, they may disagree about what stays in the budget and what should be eliminated. Often what one partner insists she needs doesn't seem sensible to the other partner and vice versa. And often what is meant by *needs* in these situations is emotional needs.

Barry knew from having worked with dozens of couples with financial strife that troubles curtailing out-of-control spending often indicate underlying emotional issues. A need to spend can be a means to avoid painful feelings of loss, sadness, and longing. Just like binge eating, drinking, or gambling, spending can bring an immediate thrill despite the later regret that may arise. Even when couples meet regularly, plan together, and create budgets, it may be impossible to stick to agreed-upon limits if one spouse is spending excessively to manage difficult feelings.

Barry knew that Grace had a long history of trying to fill a sense of emptiness by watching those infomercials on shopping channels and purchasing things they didn't need. He usually looked for some recent source of emotional distress for her that triggered the latest shopping binge. He also knew that when spouses feel more emotionally connected, they are more likely to support each other to meet financial goals—and share difficult feelings. When they feel isolated, they may look to spending to give them some satisfaction they aren't getting within their relationship. Barry's job, then, was to help Grace and James, angry as they were, better connect.

He probed a likely trigger, asking how Grace was getting along recently with her sometimes-estranged daughter, Angie. Grace immediately seemed on the verge of tears. She took a breath and said, "I try so hard, but she is always criticizing me. I can't take it and then we fight."

James seemed to understand the dynamic. "You get so hurt," he said to Grace, then looked at Barry and added, "Grace doesn't understand that Angie's just blowing off steam and she shouldn't take it so personally."

But it was more than the interaction. "When she's angry, she won't let me see her kids!" Grace responded. "I would never have disrespected my parents that way."

James reached across the couch and patted Grace's hand. "Angie will get over it," he said kindly. "I'm sure she'll be calling again soon."

Barry pointed out that if they supported each other more emotionally, they might each feel less like spending for comfort or thrills. Sharing their concerns would allow them to feel more like a team when it came to family issues, health worries, and financial planning. They nodded thoughtfully and smiled at each other.

Grace and James would need to bolster their caring connection, especially as their expenses were only going to become more challenging to manage. They agreed that having money for necessary expenses was much more important than lotion or fishing rods. But then again, maybe they'd even feel like talking about spending a little bit of money on those items that feel necessary but may not actually be.

Difficulty Finding Compromise

Derision and blame are two of the most corrosive forces in long-term relationships, according to marriage researchers John and Julie Gottman. Yet we've found that they're hard to avoid, especially for spouses struggling with financial issues. It's easy to blame each other. One spouse may have long felt comforted by the security of having money in the bank while the other may have always valued the good things in life their cash and credit could buy. As financial pressures mount, the saver may point the finger at the spender for the predicament they're now in. Or if the husband's medical bills are piling up, the wife may blame him for his health problems, saying he ignored his doctor's advice and caused their consequent financial difficulties. Or one may blame the other for not managing the money well enough or for making poor career or investment choices.

Some couples have never been big savers, accustomed to spending on whatever they want. Cutting back on expenditures to account for reduced income may be an alien and distressing notion. Others may have denied themselves possessions and experiences they fantasized about over the years and now feel entitled to fulfilling those long-held dreams. In both cases, partners may feel frustrated, resentful, and stressed about the dawning reality of their financial situation.

Sometimes they take their disappointment out on each other rather than accepting diminished economic conditions. Researchers have found that severe financial stress can strain marriages or even undermine them. Spouses with chronic money woes tend to look at each other more negatively and be more openly critical. Relieving that stress and crediting each other for whatever efforts they make toward improving their financial state allows spouses to strengthen their marriages and increase their long-term chances of surviving.

Blame, Barry believed, was aggravating James and Grace's frustration. They'd never been rich, but now they faced increasing financial concerns. In response, Grace had in fact cut way back on her spending. But James kept rubbing it in: She wasn't earning any money at all, not even a small pension. Grace felt that James blamed her for their financial problems. But she blamed him as well. Why hadn't he been motivated enough to earn more money earlier in his career? Why did he need all that hunting and fishing equipment?

Barry helped Grace and James see that blame didn't get them anywhere. It was more helpful for them to recognize that they both had real needs and emotionally driven needs and they'd both made some bad decisions. If they worked together on their finances, they could see what was left after all the spending on real needs, and they could decide together how to compromise about the items each of them wanted but didn't actually need.

Couples need to focus on their plan for the future rather than blame each other for the past. When they take the time to consider their situation, it becomes clear that they can't go back and redo past mistakes. They can only evaluate where they are and where they'll need to be and then, together, create a plan to get there.

Tying It All Together

After a little more conversation produced further mutual understanding about how they were each feeling, it was time to wrap up the session. James and Grace agreed to try to take better care of each other, talking more about their worries and supporting each other. They got up off the couch, walked a little closer together, and left the room in a far more hopeful, calmer, and happier state than they'd arrived.

How to Address Your Financial Concerns

If you and your partner have concerns about your finances and believe you could improve your money management, consider taking the following Check-Up.

You and your partner should fill out the Check-Up separately and then compare your results. There are no right or wrong answers, only places where you and your partner may have diverging or similar feelings, experiences, or needs. All are important to know about. The divergent places are opportunities to share and learn so that you can plan mindfully how you'd like to improve how you handle money in your relationship.

FINANCES CHECK-UP

1. My partner and I comfortably discuss our finances and money issues.

   Strongly Disagree   Disagree   Neutral   Agree   Strongly Agree

2. My partner and I feel that we are financially prepared for retirement.

   Strongly Disagree   Disagree   Neutral   Agree   Strongly Agree

3. My partner and I share information about our finances and agree about how they are managed.

   Strongly Disagree   Disagree   Neutral   Agree   Strongly Agree

4. My partner and I have worked hard to rid ourselves of debt.

   Strongly Disagree   Disagree   Neutral   Agree   Strongly Agree

5. My partner and I have the same values regarding money and spending.

   Strongly Disagree   Disagree   Neutral   Agree   Strongly Agree

6. My partner and I consult each other before making large purchases.

   Strongly Disagree   Disagree   Neutral   Agree   Strongly Agree

7. My partner and I believe we are both responsible with money.

   Strongly Disagree   Disagree   Neutral   Agree   Strongly Agree

8. My partner and I discuss our financial obligations to extended-family members.

   Strongly Disagree   Disagree   Neutral   Agree   Strongly Agree

9. My partner and I have up-to-date wills and healthcare proxies.

   Strongly Disagree   Disagree   Neutral   Agree   Strongly Agree

10. My partner and I agree about spending with regard to needs versus wants.

    Strongly Disagree   Disagree   Neutral   Agree   Strongly Agree

11. My partner and I have a plan for how to cut back on spending.

    Strongly Disagree   Disagree   Neutral   Agree   Strongly Agree

12. My partner and I discuss our medical needs and try to plan for unexpected expenses.

    Strongly Disagree   **Disagree**   **Neutral**   **Agree**   **Strongly Agree**

13. My partner and I don't resent each other when it comes to financial issues.

    Strongly Disagree   **Disagree**   **Neutral**   **Agree**   **Strongly Agree**

14. My partner and I agree on the lifestyle we can afford in retirement.

    Strongly Disagree   **Disagree**   **Neutral**   **Agree**   **Strongly Agree**

15. My partner and I can come to a compromise when we disagree about spending.

    Strongly Disagree   **Disagree**   **Neutral**   **Agree**   **Strongly Agree**

16. My partner and I are planning or have planned when each of us will take our Social Security.

    Strongly Disagree   **Disagree**   **Neutral**   **Agree**   **Strongly Agree**

17. My partner and I have talked to our extended-family members about our finances.

    Strongly Disagree   **Disagree**   **Neutral**   **Agree**   **Strongly Agree**

18. My partner and I have named powers of attorney in case we need help with our finances.

    Strongly Disagree   **Disagree**   **Neutral**   **Agree**   **Strongly Agree**

19. My partner and I are aware that financial strain can affect our relationship.

    Strongly Disagree   **Disagree**   **Neutral**   **Agree**   **Strongly Agree**

20. My partner and I have examined our finances together so that we both understand them.

    Strongly Disagree   **Disagree**   **Neutral**   **Agree**   **Strongly Agree**

Reviewing the Finances Check-Up

If you have five or more widely diverging answers (on opposite sides of the "neutral" choice): You probably need to address your financial issues. To best manage your financial future, you will want to express your concerns, hopes, and dreams and listen carefully to each other so that you can begin to find areas in which you agree as well as those where you'll need to compromise.

If you diverge on numbers 1, 5, or 7: You likely aren't seeing eye to eye about being responsible with your finances. Share your current thoughts and feelings about your financial situation as well as what you hope for in the future.

If you don't agree on numbers 2, 9, 10, 12, and 18: It may be time to have conversations in which you take a hard look at your current and future financial plan. You want to be prepared and know what each of you wants and needs.

If you're far apart on numbers 11, 14, 15, or 19: You may want to develop a budget that you can agree on or even get some professional financial help. See the following discussion on creating and using a budget.

Next Steps

The process we recommend is the same prescribed in the other challenges: First, listen to each other at length; problem-solve together later. It may feel slow and labored, but it's likely you haven't talked about your finances effectively with each other for a while. Try to be patient with the process; this will give you the best opportunity to fully know what your partner is thinking and feeling, and your partner will learn what you are thinking and feeling. This is an opportunity to get to know each other deeply regarding this major life concern. If you both agree to take your time with it, then you will get the most from it.

Make an appointment with each other to sit down together for an hour. You won't be making big decisions; you'll be sharing your Check-Up results and talking about where you agree and disagree. Take turns telling each other how you feel about various financial issues. Use the "Tips for Talking and Listening" found at the beginning of this book.

Let yourselves be vulnerable. Do your best to listen patiently, quietly, and nonjudgmentally. Give your partner time to talk. Remember that this isn't easy for either of you. End the hour by identifying areas of agreement from the Check-Up. Try to feel confident that you will work out your differences and reach compromises as you continue to talk together.

A Week Later

Of course, one conversation isn't enough to substantially change a decades-long relationship. Sharing your feelings, frustrations, hopes, and fears about your finances will help you feel that you are making a joint effort to be emotionally closer. You are developing a plan that will help both of you feel more secure and connected.

About a week after you discuss your Check-Up results, meet again to share any additional reactions to your findings and begin formulating a plan to improve your cooperative financial management.

Here are some questions to spur your conversation:

- What does money mean to you? Is it a reward for hard work, or does it bring a feeling of safety and security?
- What did money mean in your family growing up? What did it mean when you started to have your own money?

- If you are struggling financially now, what does it mean to work hard and then not have the freedom to spend freely on whatever you want?

- What are your hopes, goals, and intentions with your money?

- What are your fears about your finances?

- What challenges are there for you to work on a budget together?

- Are there ways that you can help each other achieve your goals regarding your finances?

- What do each of you want and need?

- Can you negotiate your financial concerns in a thoughtful, caring, cooperative way so that you both feel satisfied?

Financial struggles, unlike other challenges in the lives of couples over fifty, can be quantified in dollars and cents. If needs will remain relatively the same, couples can shift some of the money they are spending on wants to savings. They'll need to look at income, expenses, and assets and determine what works for both of them. Some couples are able to arrive at a number that suits them both. If not, they may turn to a trusted family friend or financial planner who can help them think through the consequences of their possible choices for the next ten, twenty, thirty, and even forty years.

A budget is a good place to start. This is a simple grid that tallies income and expenses. Many templates or budget worksheets are available online and can be downloaded. For example, the Budgeting Worksheet at AARP.org breaks down spousal income into such items as salaries, monthly investment income, and pension benefits; under expenses, it lists housing, utilities, food, transportation, medical, appearance (clothing, hair, etc.), and entertainment. By adding up their income and subtracting the sum of their expenses to learn their balance, spouses can find out whether they are "in the black"—taking in more money than they're spending and staying in good financial stead—or "in the red"—spending more than they're taking in and therefore going into debt.

Many websites, such as Consumer.gov, NerdWallet.com, and Payoff.com, offer guidance for creating a budget, including average percentages to spend in different categories. Or you can check with a financial planner.

Barry suggested that Grace and James create a marital financial plan. They would need to sit down and talk through their expenses, work out how much came in each month and evaluate how much had to go out. If they focused on the concrete task of creating a manageable plan, it might defuse their frustration and resentment.

Knowing how much money partners have available to spend is not enough to keep them from arguing over bills. But it's a good start. Take a month or a few months to keep track of how much you are earning, how much is in checking and savings, and how much you are spending. That will give you a foundation for creating a budget.

Like many couples, James and Grace had never kept a formal budget. They didn't know their balance but instead relied on their subjective impressions—open to frequent and heated disagreements—of whether they were spending too much or being too frugal. Working on a budget and arriving at that balance together would be an effective way of creating greater consensus about what they could truly afford. Some clients do better when they sit down together with their pile of bills and their budget worksheet once a week or every two weeks to make small and large financial decisions together. With other couples we've worked with, one person handled the bills but they both made larger budget and financial decisions together.

Of course, spouses don't always agree even then. That's when they begin negotiating about expenditures that each may want—for example, "How about I buy play tickets this month, and you purchase that new jacket the next."

Set a date to gather up your monthly bills, your assets, and your bank statements, and sit down together again. You will go through all the information together, making sure each of you has at least a basic understanding. When each of you has adequate knowledge about your financial situation, you should continue to have conversations about your finances. Go over what is important to each of you and listen to each other carefully. Begin to develop a budget that takes the needs and wishes of both of you into account as much as possible.

You may decide that meeting with a financial planner, if your budget allows, would make the process easier. A knowledgeable neutral person providing professional recommendations can ease the struggle a couple may have over control of money or debt. Whether working with an expert or alone, the goal is compromise and cooperation.

An Ongoing Plan to Integrate Change

Lasting change requires ongoing effort and fine-tuning. Schedule regular times to go over your finances and take your time to continue developing the budget. You will want to revisit it monthly at first to make sure it covers all your needs and that both of you are satisfied with it. Discuss any changes you'd like to make.

Meeting regularly to talk about money management will help you feel like a team. You'll take on financial challenges together, worry about debt together (if necessary), and enjoy the benefits of making money management a cooperative project. Your goal is to feel engaged and responsible, as a team, which can bring you closer together emotionally and give you both confidence about your future.

Steps to Success

All plans need regular review and refinement to remain fresh, relevant, and effective. Strengthen your emotional bond by doing the following:

- Pay your bills together monthly, even if one partner has always had that duty or controlled the finances. It will make both of you more aware of the details of your household economy and the ramifications of the day-to-day spending choices you make.
- Meet quarterly or twice yearly for a longer period to review your overarching financial plan.
- Keep fully informed about your financial status so your conversations are based on facts more than emotions.
- Have conversations as needed about your current and future financial goals.
- As conditions change, consider shifting your spending or income priorities to keep you on course to have the life you want with the economic security you need.

You won't likely agree on all matters, but you should be accepting and respectful as you continue to find workable compromises. Your goal is to nurture your relationship by demonstrating your care for each other as you hammer out financial challenges and decisions as a team.

Challenge 4

Infidelity

After her first few psychotherapy sessions with Carol and Ben, Julia was feeling pleased with the progress they were making in reconnecting with each other and rekindling their marriage as they adjusted to their empty-nest status. But after two months, their progress seemed to stall. Carol appeared less engaged during their sessions. Ben seemed more defensive. Julia felt they were stuck, unable or unwilling to go emotionally deeper.

When couples therapy stops progressing, it often indicates that someone is holding back. There may even be a secret—most commonly, infidelity—that hasn't been revealed. It isn't easy for a spouse to admit to making a mistake or behaving badly, and often the cheating partner is convinced it would be better to conceal the indiscretion, not wanting to hurt the spouse, suffer possible rage or retribution, or lose the relationship entirely. Sometimes, people who cheat don't even know why they engaged in behaviors that may sabotage their relationship, and, as a result, they have a hard time explaining it. Sometimes revealing infidelity and working through the fallout can feel overwhelming and unmanageable.

An important note: There is no lack of evidence about infidelity's prevalence and destructiveness among both sexes. About 20 percent of men and 13 percent of women commit adultery, according to a 2018 analysis by the University of Virginia's Institute for Family Studies. From ages eighteen to twenty-nine, men and women tend to be unfaithful at about the same rate (10 to 11 percent) and then men's rate increases greatly, whereas the increase in infidelity for women is slower. Surprisingly, both men and women are more likely to cheat later in life. Women are most likely to cheat in their sixties (16 percent); for men, it's in their seventies (26 percent).

Although she had no proof of Carol's or Ben's infidelity, Julia decided to bring up the issue at their next session.

"I know that you are working hard to rebuild your relationship," she said, "and I know you both feel you have been making progress. You've regained a lot of trust and commitment." They looked at each other and both nodded. Julia then added, "I think you're ready for the next level."

They looked at Julia, confused. Ben asked, "What is the next level?"

Good question, Julia thought. She only had a hunch. She decided to revisit their original story about their early relationship to see if either of them had had an affair that was still causing hurt and creating distance between them.

Talking about infidelity is difficult in and out of psychotherapy. There are three main issues we usually address in therapy, and usually in the same order: emotional detachment and breakdown of communication; violation of trust; and the struggle toward forgiveness and reconnection.

Emotional Detachment and Breakdown of Communication

Most psychotherapists believe axiomatically that infidelity is a sure indication that a couple has underlying difficulties with trust, communication, and mutual support. They assume that one or both spouses went looking for the emotional validation or sheer pleasure outside a marriage when they couldn't find it within the relationship. Experts assume that a sense of emotional detachment and a breakdown of communication can lay the groundwork for later infidelity. Highly publicized research from the 1990s suggested that men generally cheat because of decreased sexual satisfaction, while women cheat because of relationship dissatisfaction. But a more recent study found that relationship dissatisfaction was the cause for both genders being unfaithful.

Relationship expert Esther Perel takes a broader view. Infidelity can occur for a multitude of emotional reasons, she says. Those vulnerable to infidelity include couples who:

- Feel emotionally distant
- Avoid conflict
- Repeat the same old arguments year after year
- Have little or no sexual relationship
- Feel lonely
- Have poor communication

But, like most relationship experts, Perel also suggests that affairs can be a search for personal identity and an attempted solution to existential crises, persistent longings, and even boredom. When the spark has gone out of a relationship, an affair can make a long-frustrated spouse feel alive again.

Regardless, all therapists agree that the revelation of an affair usually prompts a marital crisis and a series of excruciating conversations about what has and hasn't worked in the relationship. Couples will need to increase their understanding of themselves and each other to begin to sort out how infidelity could have happened to them. These difficult discussions can be the beginning of a long road back to restoring a connection that has been badly damaged—or a complete severing of that bond.

When Julia questioned Ben about the early years of his relationship with Carol, he looked uncomfortable and acknowledged that he spent plenty of time with the kids but not with Carol.

"Maybe things were not really as rosy back then as we thought," Carol said. Ben stared at her.

"When we fell in love twenty-six years ago, we fell hard," she told Julia. "We were both extroverted people with career ambitions. For our first two years together, we were a power couple, invited to more parties than we had time to attend. And when we did, we enjoyed ourselves, drinking and using recreational drugs sometimes until the morning. Our sex life was intense, frequent, and passionate." She took a breath and looked over at Ben. He nodded, looking uncomfortable.

Carol went on. "When we decided to start a family, we were approaching thirty and my interest in partying had definitely waned. I was working long hours as a corporate attorney. Ben was moving up the food chain from sales to management and continued to enjoy doing business deals over multiple bottles of expensive wine.

"Ben continued to work late, come home drunk, and want sex pretty often," Carol continued. She, meanwhile, was a mom with young kids.

Ben helped a little with the kids and, as they grew older, bonded with them over sports. "But," he said, "I wasn't really paying attention to Carol like I should have."

Julia listened intently, knowing that relationship incompatibility is a frequent rationalization for infidelity. Spouses don't feel connected enough, don't share values, and don't feel like they're on the same team.

Carol's voice became quieter as she continued: "After the twins were born, I had been comfortably sober for more than a year and was focused on being the best mom I could be. But Ben continued to party. I knew it was part of his job to wine and dine people, so I bit my tongue."

Ben nodded. "It's true," he said with a touch of sadness.

Carol looked at Julia and said, "It isn't like he had a great role model. His dad was never home when he was growing up."

So, Julia thought, Ben may have always had problems maintaining closeness, and their different lifestyles in those years may have pulled them slowly apart. Young spouses, wrapped up in demanding jobs and hanging out with friends, may not recognize the value of attending to their relationship. They may take each other for granted. Once that distance sets in, they may no longer look to each other for emotional support and may avoid sensitive conversations. Their communication may even become superficial and impersonal. This lack of intimacy can impact their sex life as well.

Not surprisingly, that's what happened with Carol and Ben. She admitted using menopause as an excuse for their lack of sex, but it wasn't completely true.

Ben interrupted, "I was trying then, but you just wouldn't give me a chance. I felt rejected by you all the time."

Caught in a relationship without enough emotional closeness and sexual excitement, partners may stray outside their marriage in search of them.

Violation of Trust

By the time the girls were about five, Ben continued to stay out late a lot, continuing to wine and dine as part of his job.

"I suspected he was having affairs," said Carol. "He'd stopped wanting sex so frequently. Mostly I felt relieved. But I also felt lonely."

Julia turned to Ben: "Do you want to confirm or deny anything Carol said?"

Before he could answer, Carol interrupted to say, "By the time the children were teens, I had begun talking to Jack, a man who did landscaping work for us. It was nothing at first, just friendly conversation. It felt nice to talk to someone who listened and seemed to care." Carol rushed on with the story. "I began to look forward to these conversations a little too eagerly. And then we were making out. And then, you know, we were having a fling."

Ben looked at her with disbelief. "You got involved with the yard guy?" he asked incredulously. "I can't believe it." He paused and then said angrily, "I feel like a fool."

Carol looked at him and said, "I'm sorry. I guess I just needed some closeness with someone. I couldn't get that from you. The affair fizzled out pretty quickly."

Julia sat with them silently while they both were quiet for a long time, letting the revelation sink in. Then Ben looked down and said in a low voice more sad than angry, "It's not like I didn't betray you, too."

When unfaithfulness is revealed, the injured party typically feels lied to, misled, and completely betrayed, as if the trust on which her relationship was built has been violated. She may wonder if she even wants to try to ever trust her partner again. Viewing this couple from the outside, it will seem obvious that the partner who cheated is fully responsible for the adultery. This, of course, is true. One partner cannot be blamed for the other partner's behavior.

But, as noted earlier, infidelity is not just about someone having an affair. It generally means that something is amiss within the couple's relationship. Whether it represents a long-standing emotional disconnect, years of unspoken resentment, sexual concerns, old trauma, or some other hard-to-deal-with issue, its causes are often deeper than lust and adventure seeking.

Many spouses who have had affairs wonder if it would really be for the best to reveal the truth. In a *Psychology Today* blog post titled "Should You Tell Your Partner You Cheated?," Robert Weiss, PhD, MSW, claims there may be good reasons at times to keep an affair a secret, although he recommends that cheaters come clean if they want to have a healthy relationship. The most obvious reason not to tell the truth is when there's no intention to repair the relationship. Or if the guilty party is afraid his partner is too emotionally or physically fragile to cope with the revelation. Or if he fears that any information he offers will one day be used against him in divorce court. When the affair he'd gotten away with has been long over, keeping mum about it now may feel to him like the safest bet.

Even when betrayed spouses don't have any idea about the violation, they are likely to notice some greater emotional distance in their marriage. As Weiss reports, many of them blame themselves for this lack of closeness. Then again, there are spouses who would rather not know about the infidelity because they don't want to disrupt the family, hurt their kids, or become the topic of neighborhood gossip.

As Ben continued to look sad, Carol spontaneously moved closer to him and slowly touched him on the shoulder. "Thank you for saying that," she said. "I knew, but it means a lot that you are telling me the truth.

"We have both done stupid, hurtful things."

Struggle Toward Forgiveness and Reconnection

When admitting to infidelity, the cheating partner needs to prove that he wants to repair his relationship. He must end his affair, if it isn't already over. And he must accept full responsibility for his actions. Then he will need to patiently give his partner room to recover.

Whether the relationship can recover after an affair depends on each partner's ability to listen without judgment or assumptions.

Spouses working to repair their relationship may feel that they've discussed the feelings of betrayal and lost trust many times before and they just want to move on. But if one partner remains unsatisfied, then the issues must be revisited again and again until both are at peace. This can take time and patience; there is no shortcut. If couples don't make the time to do this, it is likely they will continue to feel disconnected. Often, when going over the betrayal continues to be an issue, one partner isn't feeling adequately reassured about the current level of trust and commitment from the other partner.

Moving forward from infidelity is extremely challenging for couples, even when both claim to be committed to preserving their marriage. Once basic trust has been shattered, the relationship could be beyond repair. John Gottman, a noted marriage researcher and leader in the field of couples therapy, describes the series of complex steps couples must go through in an effort to recover from infidelity: atonement, attunement, and attachment. Recognizing the painful and sometimes-traumatic impact an affair can have is the first step. Facing previously avoided conflicts and aligning emotional understanding comes next. Repairing and strengthening attachment is the third phase of his therapeutic process.

Julia looked closely at Ben and Carol, sitting side by side, both in their own pain. Would they eventually be able to forgive each other? Facing betrayal and restoring trust wasn't going to be easy. "You've both done such hard work to repair your relationship," she said. "I think getting past these old betrayals will be what brings you closer to each other."

Sometimes, an affair can lead to positive change. As psychotherapist Michele Weiner-Davis writes in her book *Healing from Infidelity*, "Many clients have shared that had it not been for their partner's affair, they'd never have looked at, discussed, and healed some of the under-lying issues that were broken at the foundation of their relationship."

Julia looked at Ben and Carol sympathetically and added, "I can see that there's more work for you to do. But you've made some major progress today."

Julia reflected on whether Ben and Carol would be able to work through their betrayals. Although couples therapy has been found to be about 75 percent effective for saving long-term relationships, cou-ples struggling with adultery were twice as likely to be divorced five years after therapy as those coping with other marital problems. But 57 percent of those who revealed their cheating during therapy were still married after five years, one study points out, versus 20 percent of those who kept their affairs secret. At least now, by revealing their affairs to each other, Ben and Carol had almost tripled their chances of surviving as a couple.

Tying It All Together

After several more sessions working through their painful revela-tions, Ben and Carol sat down on Julia's couch to report on their efforts. Julia had recommended that they remember what their early, passionate relationship felt like and go on dates. On their first night out, after a glass of wine at a candlelit table, Ben leaned over for a kiss, and Carol burst out laughing. His feelings were immediately hurt, but he pulled himself together, remembering how they had talked in couples therapy about tolerating each other's anxiety. "I apologized for my nervous laughter," said Carol, "and we finished up a friendly dinner together."

On their second date night, Carol wore a pair of earrings that Ben had bought her for her birthday. They held hands in the car on the way to the restaurant. They both felt committed to rekindling their relationship now.

At the end of the dinner, she kissed him and no one laughed.

How to Address Your Infidelity Concerns

If you and your partner have concerns about infidelity, whether in the distant past or more recent, and feel that your relationship could use some improvement with regard to trust and connection, consider taking the following Check-Up.

You and your partner should fill out the Check-Up separately and with as much honesty and transparency as possible. Addressing infidelity issues can be difficult because acknowledging mistakes will likely be experienced as a betrayal of trust and can therefore feel especially risky. But if you both want to improve your relationship, it is important to be open and honest. Continuing to keep secrets will interfere with your efforts to feel closer. Each of you should agree in advance that, whatever the results, you are committed to making the effort to work through them. Then compare those results. There are no right or wrong answers, only places where you and your partner may have diverging or similar feelings, experiences, or needs. All are important to know about. The divergent places are opportunities to share and learn so that you can plan mindfully how to cope with infidelity, trust, and loyalty issues.

INFIDELITY CHECK-UP

1. My partner and I completely trust that we will always be faithful to each other.

   Strongly Disagree   **Disagree**   **Neutral**   **Agree**   **Strongly Agree**

2. My partner and I have the same values regarding infidelity.

   Strongly Disagree   **Disagree**   **Neutral**   **Agree**   **Strongly Agree**

3. My partner and I wouldn't be surprised to learn that the other had cheated.

   Strongly Disagree   **Disagree**   **Neutral**   **Agree**   **Strongly Agree**

4. My partner and I don't have lingering feelings about past infidelity.

   Strongly Disagree   **Disagree**   **Neutral**   **Agree**   **Strongly Agree**

5. My partner and I focus on the here and now regarding our commitment to each other.

   Strongly Disagree   **Disagree**   **Neutral**   **Agree**   **Strongly Agree**

6. My partner and I have truly forgiven each other for past breaches of any kind.

   Strongly Disagree   **Disagree**   **Neutral**   **Agree**   **Strongly Agree**

7. My partner and I have talked through everything we need to about past infidelity.

   Strongly Disagree   **Disagree**   **Neutral**   **Agree**   **Strongly Agree**

8. My partner and I are both sorry for how we've treated each other in the past.

   Strongly Disagree   **Disagree**   **Neutral**   **Agree**   **Strongly Agree**

9. My partner and I need to work harder to move on from past mistakes.

   Strongly Disagree   **Disagree**   **Neutral**   **Agree**   **Strongly Agree**

10. My partner and I take the time to be together and feel connected.

    Strongly Disagree   Disagree   Neutral   Agree   Strongly Agree

11. My partner and I would tell each other if we felt an irresistible attraction to someone else.

    Strongly Disagree   Disagree   Neutral   Agree   Strongly Agree

12. My partner and I keep our sex life exciting, even after all these years.

    Strongly Disagree   Disagree   Neutral   Agree   Strongly Agree

13. My partner and I feel close to each other most of the time.

    Strongly Disagree   Disagree   Neutral   Agree   Strongly Agree

14. My partner and I would feel devastated if we learned that the other had cheated.

    Strongly Disagree   Disagree   Neutral   Agree   Strongly Agree

15. My partner and I can tell each other what we prefer sexually.

    Strongly Disagree   Disagree   Neutral   Agree   Strongly Agree

16. My partner and I would be willing to work through infidelity to preserve our relationship.

    Strongly Disagree   Disagree   Neutral   Agree   Strongly Agree

17. My partner and I would divorce if we learned that one of us had cheated.

    Strongly Disagree   Disagree   Neutral   Agree   Strongly Agree

18. My partner and I are willing to discuss what it would take to restore trust.

    Strongly Disagree   Disagree   Neutral   Agree   Strongly Agree

19. My partner and I know it would take a long time to restore trust.

    Strongly Disagree   Disagree   Neutral   Agree   Strongly Agree

20. My partner and I feel we get all our sexual needs met with each other.

    Strongly Disagree   Disagree   Neutral   Agree   Strongly Agree

Reviewing the Infidelity Check-Up

If you differ by two or more degrees on 1, 2, 3, 14, or 19: Make some time to discuss your level of trust in each other and what you can do together to strengthen it. Building trust back into your relationship is a foundational part of improving your connection and recovering a sense of closeness.

If you differ on 4, 6, 7, 8, or 9: You and your partner may need to revisit old hurts and feelings of betrayal, to have a focused conversation about where you each are, and to discuss how to move forward from there. Even if only one of you feels the need to revisit the past, you will need to do so together, as often as it takes to peacefully leave it behind.

If you differ on 5, 10, 11, 12, 13, or 20: You'll need to discuss whether you both are truly committed to working out a better relationship now and going forward. If you are not seeing eye to eye, you'll want to explore what is preventing that process. You may need to consult a couples therapist to work through your concerns.

Next Steps

Our suggestions for facing the challenges posed by infidelity use the same framework as described in the previous challenge. First, we recommend a long and intensive listening session. This can be more complicated with infidelity than with other major life challenges because basic trust has been damaged. After enough time has elapsed for you to emotionally process and reflect on the first conversation's exchange, a concerted problem-solving session should follow.

The listening process may feel slow and labored, but it's absolutely necessary for you to move forward together. Try to be patient with the process; this will give you the best opportunity to fully know what your partner is thinking and feeling, and your partner will learn what you are thinking and feeling. This is an opportunity to get to know each other deeply regarding this major life challenge. If you both agree to take your time with it, then you will get the most from it.

Make an appointment to sit down together for an hour. You won't be making big decisions; you'll be sharing your Check-Up results and talking about where you agree and disagree. Take turns telling each other how you feel about your infidelity and trust issues. Use the "Tips for Talking and Listening" found at the beginning of this book.

Remember that your goal is to feel more connected. End the hour by identifying areas of agreement from the Check-Up and setting a positive goal, such as working on a project around the house together or planning a romantic date. This will be an opportunity to feel closer.

A Week Later

About a week after you discuss your Check-Up results, meet again to share any additional reactions to your findings and begin formulating a plan to work through your feelings about infidelity, past or recent, and build trust and closeness. Take your time to explore the areas from the Check-Up where you connect and share values. Even when there are past mistakes, couples can learn from them to build a stronger connection going forward if they commit to making the effort. Reinforce areas that you agree on, and explore areas in which you do not share the same view. Try to understand your differences rather than react to them.

Discuss actions that will make it easier to keep the mistakes in the past and prevent them from interfering in your current relationship.

Here are some questions to spur your conversation:

- Does the partner who had an affair feel genuine remorse? Without it, trust can't be restored nor can healing begin.

- Are you both committed to addressing your issues with honesty and openness?

- Is the partner who was betrayed capable of considering forgiveness? This may take time and continued openness and trust building, but without it, the relationship will never move beyond resentment.

- Does one partner require reassurance that the other is loyal? What could support that? Access to each other's electronic devices, including passwords and social media accounts? Openness about each other's whereabouts when you are apart?

- Would affectionate attention help maintain confidence in the relationship?

- Are you both willing to make a plan to spend time together engaged in something that you both value to build connection?

- What will help each of you rebuild your trust and intimacy?

- What do each of you want and need within your relationship?

- Can you negotiate your issues in a thoughtful, caring, cooperative way so that you both feel satisfied?

An Ongoing Plan to Integrate Change

When there has been a betrayal, fully integrating change can take a long time. Plan to meet again for as many times as necessary to talk about how you both feel about what has happened and about the levels of trust and commitment in your relationship. We stress this again: Even if only one of you feels the need to talk about the infidelity, you both need to make the time to do so. Your goal is to continue to be there for each other and to improve your feelings of connection and trust.

We have found that sharing feelings, even the difficult ones, brings couples closer, increases their knowledge of each other, and leads to a greater sense of trust. Even when you are frustrated, using the preceding list of conversation points can help you work through your issues to get to an increased level of mutual understanding and closeness. Usually it's the most difficult conversations that ultimately lead to the greatest sense of satisfaction.

When you disagree about anything along the way, you should both remember to accept and respect each other as you continue to work on your changing relationship. Your ultimate goal is to make your relationship stronger and better than it was before. The secret to achieving that goal is to build in more trust and emotional connection.

Steps to Success

If infidelity has been an issue in your relationship, your ultimate goal is to rebuild the relationship so that it is stronger moving forward. Keep the following steps in mind as you go.

- Strengthen your emotional bond by sharing feelings and setting aside times to talk about those difficult feelings, past and present.
- Always try to listen without judgment. Trust and betrayal are not easy to talk about.
- Make honesty and openness a priority.
- Plan date nights and other activities together and pursue new experiences.
- Share what each of you needs from the other.
- Have conversations about the future.

Can you both commit to take the time and make the effort to do the necessary work together to be successful? Ultimately, having conversations about infidelity will bring you closer together if you are truly committed to working through this challenging issue. Rebuilding comfort and trust can be a long, hard process. Staying committed to it can bring your marriage to a level of closeness and intimacy that you may never have experienced before. The fulfillment you will feel from your new and improved relationship is worth every moment of effort.

If you aren't making progress working through the betrayal and trust issues on your own, you may consider seeking help from a couples therapist. Many people find it helpful to begin to deal with these delicate, sensitive issues with some guidance.

Retirement

Elaine shrieked, "I can't stand it!" Then she covered her mouth and apologized to Julia. She'd come in for an appointment without Phil to talk about how retirement was going for them.

"Not so well, I take it," Julia replied.

Elaine was clearly unhappy. As she explained to Julia, it felt like Phil had taken over the house. She was worried that he'd have another heart attack—he'd had one five years earlier—sitting around eating chips and watching golf on TV half the day. She thought he'd always valued being active and working hard, and now she was frustrated watching him sit on the couch with the remote, doing nothing.

It wasn't that she had no sympathy for him. He'd retired two months earlier, after climbing the career ladder at a major manufacturing company and reaching the position of operations manager, where he'd stayed for fifteen years. He relished having no alarm clock, no dress clothes and briefcase, no rush hour, no deadlines, and no kowtowing to top executives. He'd gotten a decent retirement package, and they had enough savings. But she had retired when he did, and now they were home together. While retirement made him happy, it made her irritable and impatient. This was not what she'd expected. She enjoyed spending more time with Hope and the grandchildren—happily settled into a condo nearby. But she'd also imagined travel, new projects, and a sense of adventure.

Over forty-three million people are retired now, and more than seventy-five million Americans will retire in the next decade. For many, leaving the workforce affects their self-identity, self-worth, and feelings about what makes life meaningful. They struggle with what to do with their time. They worry about finances. They don't plan ahead to make those retirement years as successful as they had envisioned them.

To make this more complicated, fewer than 20 percent of partners retire in the same year, according to the Center for Retirement Research at Boston College. That means that most spouses are not coordinating their retirements together. They may not be sharing their hopes and fears about postwork life, much less their plans for their daily lives and their finances. They may not be planning their future in close deliberation with each other at all. Their assumption that retirement will just fall into place naturally is often misguided. An Ameriprise Financial survey found that almost 70 percent of those surveyed between ages sixty and seventy-three had trouble initially adapting to retirement.

It's as if the couples who painstakingly sampled hors d'oeuvres for their wedding, chose a house to buy, timed the birth of their kids, and plotted career strategies feel like they're off the hook after the last day of employment. Retirement is a blank canvas they imagine they'll fill in as they go along and try out a little bit of this and a little bit of that. But it doesn't usually work out well.

Instead, we recommend that couples take the same planful stance toward this life phase, setting aside time to share their thoughts and feelings about retirement. How will it impact their relationship? (It will.) How will children and other family members react? (They'll be affected, too.) Through re-creating life together, will they put themselves on a path toward deeper appreciation and gratitude? (Only if they've taken careful steps beforehand.) In our work with couples over fifty, we've learned that the sweeping changes during the retirement transition are best handled with well-thought-out planning and abundant patience.

If they are, those long-term relationships can thrive during retirement. Couples adapt to this life transition with increased zest for living and passion for each other. But for couples who haven't planned well, misunderstandings can lead to elevated stress, not greater relaxation. So let us walk you through how you can start planning now—whether you're already retired or thinking of it—mustering your patience and focusing on the three major areas that we've found can lead you to a successful retirement: expectations, balancing We Time and Me Time, and finding meaning.

Expectations

We've found that when couples retire without planning together, they may not even be aware that they have different—often radically different—expectations. But a lack of planning can lead to the strong possibility that their respective expectations will be mismatched in important areas. This, in turn, can lead to increased tension and discontent.

When couples don't retire at the same time, the spouse who is still working may expect that the household chores will be redistributed with more responsibility given to the retired spouse to make dinner, run errands, and pay bills. But have those shifts been spelled out and agreed upon? Or is the retiree assuming that she is retiring from household duties as well, much to the annoyance of a still-busy partner?

Even when couples do retire at the same time, one spouse may feel that the division of chores will naturally remain the same, while the other may have very different expectations.

Chores aren't the only area of divergent expectations. Like others who transition to retirement, Elaine missed the social connections she'd had at work. But she had at least developed other social outlets over the years: the gym, her book club, and volunteer work. Like many men, Phil had focused on his career, and almost all his social needs were met through his job and family. He now felt isolated, and he depended more on Elaine for companionship. He had little to do with his time. They hadn't discussed their expectations for sharing time together—and time apart. The Ameriprise Financial survey found that more than a third of retirees missed socializing with work colleagues.

Lack of discussion set up Phil and Elaine for a retirement impasse. He had counted down the years to retirement, which in his mind meant R&R. Elaine had imagined retirement as a time for adventures, travel, extended family, and new pursuits. "A little excitement, a little romance," as she put it. She wanted to be with him more, but now she could see nothing for their future except having to watch Phil grow older and weaker in the TV's white glare. He expected her to make his meals, do his laundry, and keep the house clean, just as she always had. She was still busy, though, and was ready to share the chores. She and Phil were not on the same page. But they were stuck in the same house, on edge.

Like many couples, retirement wasn't going the way either Phil or Elaine had imagined. They were both surprised to find they had more conflict now than before they'd retired. How was it that they'd never talked about their expectations for this stage of their lives?

In contrast, another couple who consulted with Barry had planned their retirement schedule so thoroughly that it felt as if they were leaving one set of jobs for another. They had jumped right into a series of activities including a kitchen renovation, courses at the local college, and a series of gym classes and personal training that they'd been eagerly anticipating for years. But they found themselves feeling over-whelmed rather than relaxed and happy. Barry helped them take a step back to reevaluate their priorities so that they had some time and space to process this big transition in their lives. Ultimately, they worked through a schedule readjustment and found better balance.

Balancing We Time and Me Time

More free time in retirement offers many possibilities but also, again, potential conflicts. More than a third of retirees said they found adjusting to a new daily routine challenging. Spouses need to negotiate a mutually acceptable plan about how time will be spent together and apart. Their priorities may turn out to be quite different.

Miriam Goodman, author of *Too Much Togetherness: Surviving Retirement as a Couple*, has found that the biggest issue for spouses when they retire is having too much time together. Most haven't considered how long stretches of days in each other's company could affect their relationship. They assume that more time together will be more fun and lead to a greater sense of closeness. Often, it's what they've longed for over the years. But when that retirement comes, for many couples, more time can mean more discord.

No two people have exactly the same need for time together and time apart. Finding a comfortable balance of We Time and Me Time—time spent with each other and time spent on their own pursuits—is crucial for a peaceful retirement. Couples may have to renegotiate this balance frequently as conditions change.

Elaine and Phil certainly needed to find their comfort zone. After Elaine's individual session with Julia, they both came in to air their feelings and figure out how to make retirement work for both of them. When Julia suggested that they discuss how much time they'd like to spend together and apart, they were surprised that it hadn't occurred to them to do that before they retired.

Elaine quickly realized that she hadn't planned for herself. She missed having a schedule. Despite her activities and occasional baby-sitting for the grandkids, she still had too much free time, and when she was home, there sat Phil on the couch. It felt like she and Phil were wasting time now, waiting for something.

Phil, on the other hand, loved the feeling of having open time ahead of him with nothing to do—at first. He resisted building a schedule. But as time passed, and he and Elaine met with Julia periodically, his feelings changed. After he'd been retired for about six months, he began to feel bored. Or was it depressed? He wasn't exercising. Days went by when he hardly spoke to anyone except Elaine. He had no reason to get dressed. Sometimes he didn't bother showering. He'd gone from busy, stressed, and active to stagnant. It started dawning on him that perhaps a little structure wouldn't hurt.

Most retirement experts recommend that couples view the transition to retirement as an opportunity to renegotiate a variety of aspects of their relationship, including how they spend their time. How much time together do we each want? Time apart? Spouses need to propose activities that they want to share or do alone. They need to speak up honestly when their partner asks them to do activities they don't want to do. Most couples benefit from planning ahead. On the other hand, you may want to avoid cramming too much into the schedule, since one of the joys of retirement can be the opportunity for spontaneity.

We often recommend that our clients build into their schedule regular exercise—critical for health as well as an opportunity for togetherness. Some couples exercise together in the morning, talking about their upcoming day or week. Participation in a sport or attending classes at the gym can widen your social circle. Whatever activities you choose, aim for a flexible schedule, including time together and apart, time alone and with friends and family, time doing meaningful activities, time trying out new pursuits apart or together, and some downtime with nothing on the horizon.

Elaine and Phil decided to hit the gym together three times a week—an increase from never for Phil and with room enough for Elaine to continue to go to her classes with friends on two or three other days. The gym was, she admitted, her suggestion. But he responded positively—to her relief.

Finding Meaning

Research indicates that one of the best predictors of health and happiness in retirement is meaningful pursuits that replace the sense of purpose many retirees derived from their previous work life. That doesn't necessarily mean volunteering at the soup kitchen or animal shelter—although it can. And couples don't necessarily have to find meaning in the same way. What's important is that they share their hopes for the future and discover what has value for each of them as well as what they may find meaningful together.

Does retirement mean the same thing to both partners? For some, it's a quieter time to slow down and withdraw from activities and relationships that don't give them much enjoyment. For others, it's a time to gear up with more pursuits and opportunities to engage with others through social gatherings, exercise groups, classes, and exotic trips. It's not always easy to have a deliberate talk about finding meaning and supporting each other if your approaches differ. Is there a middle ground you can both occupy and where you can grow together?

What makes a pursuit meaningful? Meaning can take many forms. Yes, you can sign up together to serve meals and sort clothes at the local shelter, or clean kennel cages. Or you may sign up for a language class or audit a college course. Start a small business or begin a second career. Get more involved in your spiritual community. Partners who take part in activities such as these feel connected to others and something larger than themselves. They wake up each day with focus and drive. They feel like they can still make a difference. According to research, participating in interesting new activities leads to increased well-being, self-worth, and self-esteem, as well as improved couples' relationships.

Elaine and Phil both came to feel that something was lacking in their lives as they progressed through their first year of retirement. They realized that they needed something to replace the self-worth and value that they'd derived from their jobs. And they needed some excitement and a few challenges in their schedule. So they intentionally tried to build meaning into their retirement lives. Elaine was the planner in the family, so she gradually added activities to their weekly calendar with Phil's okay. She planned a weekly date night at new restaurants. She scheduled chores, like yard work, that they could do together. She set aside time for weekly visits with the grandkids. When a friend of Phil's from work called to see how he was doing, they made plans for the two couples to go out to dinner.

Elaine read about a new program for volunteers to read to underprivileged children at the library. She thought it would be something they could do together. Phil agreed to try it. She knew he wouldn't be sorry.

Tying It All Together

Phil and Elaine divvied up the household chores, reaching a workable compromise, and agreed to regularly review the plan. They were mindful to leave plenty of unstructured time so they could act spontaneously.

Phil still had plenty of time to sink into the couch and watch golf, but he was also pleased with his gym schedule, social outings, and volunteer activities. And Elaine enjoyed her time with Phil and had time to get together with her girlfriends. And there were those babysitting opportunities. With their schedule of time together and apart, plans and downtime, and meaningful activities, they were finally adjusting to retirement well. Both were able to do what they wanted most of the time and felt satisfied that they could renegotiate together as their circumstances and interests changed over time. They both had begun to truly enjoy their retirement.

How to Address Your Retirement Concerns

If you or your partner—or both of you—are contemplating retirement, or are already retired, consider taking the following Check-Up.

You and your partner should fill out the Check-Up separately and then compare your results. There are no right or wrong answers, only places where you and your partner may have diverging or similar feelings, experiences, or needs. All are important to know about. The divergent places are opportunities to share and learn so that you can plan mindfully how you'd like your retirement to be.

RETIREMENT CHECK-UP

1. My partner and I agree on how to prioritize our expenses.

   Strongly Disagree   **Disagree**   **Neutral**   **Agree**   **Strongly Agree**

2. My partner and I agree about when we will each retire.

   Strongly Disagree   **Disagree**   **Neutral**   **Agree**   **Strongly Agree**

3. My partner and I have decided when each of us will begin to take Social Security.

   Strongly Disagree   **Disagree**   **Neutral**   **Agree**   **Strongly Agree**

4. My partner and I have discussed our plans for retirement.

   Strongly Disagree   **Disagree**   **Neutral**   **Agree**   **Strongly Agree**

5. My partner and I agree about the amount of time we spend together and apart.

   Strongly Disagree   **Disagree**   **Neutral**   **Agree**   **Strongly Agree**

6. My partner and I have some interests in common and plan to pursue them together.

   Strongly Disagree   **Disagree**   **Neutral**   **Agree**   **Strongly Agree**

7. My partner and I have some different interests that we pursue separately.

   Strongly Disagree   **Disagree**   **Neutral**   **Agree**   **Strongly Agree**

8. My partner and I share equitably in the household chores.

   Strongly Disagree   **Disagree**   **Neutral**   **Agree**   **Strongly Agree**

9. My partner and I agree about where we will live in retirement.

   Strongly Disagree   **Disagree**   **Neutral**   **Agree**   **Strongly Agree**

10. My partner and I agree about how much time we spend with extended family.

    Strongly Disagree   **Disagree**   **Neutral**   **Agree**   **Strongly Agree**

11. My partner and I agree about how much financial support we give to extended family.

Strongly Disagree   **Disagree**   **Neutral**   **Agree**   **Strongly Agree**

12. My partner and I communicate well and feel close to each other.

Strongly Disagree   **Disagree**   **Neutral**   **Agree**   **Strongly Agree**

13. My partner and I have definite plans for activities we like to do together and apart.

Strongly Disagree   **Disagree**   **Neutral**   **Agree**   **Strongly Agree**

14. My partner and I talk about how we feel about retirement.

Strongly Disagree   **Disagree**   **Neutral**   **Agree**   **Strongly Agree**

15. My partner and I have always enjoyed spending time together.

Strongly Disagree   **Disagree**   **Neutral**   **Agree**   **Strongly Agree**

16. My partner and I discuss our hopes and dreams.

Strongly Disagree   **Disagree**   **Neutral**   **Agree**   **Strongly Agree**

17. My partner and I care similarly about being near friends and family.

Strongly Disagree   **Disagree**   **Neutral**   **Agree**   **Strongly Agree**

18. My partner and I allow each other to meet our social needs.

Strongly Disagree   **Disagree**   **Neutral**   **Agree**   **Strongly Agree**

19. My partner and I encourage each other to try new things.

Strongly Disagree   **Disagree**   **Neutral**   **Agree**   **Strongly Agree**

20. My partner and I feel like a team with regard to retirement years.

Strongly Disagree   **Disagree**   **Neutral**   **Agree**   **Strongly Agree**

Reviewing the Retirement Check-Up

If you have five or more widely diverging answers (on opposite sides of the "neutral" choice): You probably need to address your retirement concerns. You probably haven't shared your views and feelings about retirement enough to reach common ground.

If your answers are on opposite sides of neutral for 2, 3, 4, 9, 13, or 16: You have not planned for the future enough together. Take time to discuss your hopes, dreams, and plans for what's next.

If your answers diverge on 5, 6, 7, 8, or 10: You have some negotiating to do over time spent together, apart, with family, and with others. Start by sharing your preferences about these concerns and listening carefully without judgment.

If your answers diverge on 12, 14, and 20: You may have to put special effort into communicating about your feelings.

Next Steps

The following process may feel slow and labored, but it's likely that you could benefit by committing time and effort to hashing out together the many important aspects that contribute to successful retirement. Try to be patient with this process; it will give you the best opportunity to fully know what your partner is thinking and feeling, and your partner will learn what you are thinking and feeling. This is an opportunity to deeply explore each other's hopes and dreams with regard to retirement. Retirement is a major life transition that many people underestimate. It can bring up feelings of loss, fear, discomfort, and other difficult emotions. It can also be the opportunity of a lifetime to start anew, explore exciting new activities, and find new meaning together and apart. If you both agree to take your time with it, you will get the most from it.

Make an appointment with each other to sit down together for an hour. You won't be making big decisions; you'll be sharing your Check-Up results and talking about where you agree and disagree. Take turns telling each other how you feel about this big life transition. Use the "Tips for Talking and Listening" found at the beginning of this book. You'll be surprised to learn what your partner has in mind or hasn't yet considered. Let yourselves be vulnerable. Do your best to listen patiently, quietly, and nonjudgmentally. Give your partner time to talk. Remember that this may not be easy for either of you. Change is hard. Try to explore all the possibilities that you can think of between you so that you can jointly make the best, most fulfilling plans for the future.

Remember that your goal is to feel more connected. End the hour by identifying areas of agreement from the Check-Up and setting a positive goal, such as exploring a retirement pursuit together. This will be an opportunity to feel closer.

A Week Later

About a week after you discuss your Check-Up results, meet again to share any additional reactions to your findings and begin formulating a plan to improve your relationship. Continue to share your hopes, dreams, and fears about retirement. The goal is for it to be the best that it can be, given whatever constraints the two of you bring to the picture.

Here are some questions to spur your conversation:

- How do you feel about retirement?
- What are you hoping for, day-to-day and in the long run, in retirement?

- What will be meaningful to you?
- How do you feel about your finances?
- What worries you about retirement?
- How much time would you ideally like to have together, apart, with your immediate family, with your extended family, and with friends?
- What areas of interest and meaning do you agree on and how would you like to pursue them?
- How will you manage diverging goals for postwork life?
- How can you help each other achieve your goals?
- What do each of you want and need?

Make a plan to spend time together engaged in activities you both value, and time apart to pursue your individual interests. Reflect on your experiences and continue to share your feelings, hopes, and dreams.

An Ongoing Plan to Integrate Change

While planning for retirement, or once you are retired, you'll want to check in as many times as you both deem necessary to continue to talk about your hopes and dreams for the future. Talk about your plans to take care of yourselves through the retirement process and how you both feel about your visions of the retirement years now that you have been talking them through. Continue to have conversations about these issues as time passes and unexpected changes occur. Create a schedule you can work with. Along the way, you'll make adjustments and compromise to work together as a couple to make the retirement years as good as they can be. You should continue to accept and respect your partner as you work on your changing relationship. Your goal is to feel more connected, to support each other to fulfill your dreams, and to find meaning as you travel through this new phase of life. Remember to continue to share feelings, experiences, and even grief to keep your relationship as strong and healthy as possible.

Steps to Success

We have found that couples frequently avoid discussing retirement. Worries about when to retire, how, where, and what's next often remain unexpressed. Such a big life transition can bring up anxious feelings about the future, health, money, and many other issues. We recommend that couples talk about retirement early and frequently.

Keep the following steps in mind as you go.

- Discuss your ongoing expectations for the future.
- Manage your time together and apart.
- Periodically discuss finances to enjoy the present and plan for the future.
- Search together and separately to find meaning in new pursuits.
- Check in when changes occur in your lives.

Retirement is an opportunity for both of you to grow together and separately. Exploring new interests and pursuits and increasing your sense of purpose and your feelings of connection will create meaning in this new and exciting phase of your life.

Challenge 6

Downsizing and Relocating

Downsizing would be a huge challenge when Elaine and Phil eventually moved, but that wasn't what had brought Elaine back to Julia's couch. Phil absolutely refused to consider leaving the turn-of-the-century three-story brick home where they had lived for more than thirty years.

Elaine understood his reluctance. They shared a multitude of memories of their children and grandchildren wreaking havoc in practically every room. Over the decades, they had filled the house with photos as well as art and furnishings they had chosen with love. Leaving would be emotionally devastating.

But it was time. Since Phil's double knee replacement last year, he seemed unsteady. Watching him go up and down the stairs, even while holding on to the heavy wooden banister, Elaine was afraid he might slip and fall. They had to move to a place without stairs, and they were at that age when they had to think about what they'd need in the coming years.

In our work, we've found that downsizing and relocating can be stressful and even traumatic. It can coincide with other difficult life transitions such as job loss, retirement, divorce, or the death of a spouse. Even when it is a choice, it can be hard because the comfort we feel at home is crucial to our well-being. Besides the structure itself, we all have our own sense of what makes a place a home: our community of friends, shop owners and neighbors who know us, schools and playgrounds where our children grew up. When we downsize and relocate, we can feel like we are leaving behind the lives we've led.

According to a 2019 Merrill Lynch Retirement study, 64 percent of retirees have moved or anticipate moving in retirement: 29 percent to be closer to their families and 26 percent to cut down on their expenses. Of those who decide not to move, their main reason is that they love their homes.

No wonder. Attachments to home, neighbors, nearby family and friends, and community and religious institutions, built over many years, can be powerful. Anxieties about relocation can feel paralyzing. Moving "can feel like you are letting go of a particular part of your life," says Dr. David Mischoulon, director of the Depression Clinical and Research Program at Massachusetts General Hospital. "There's a realization that you can't get the past back."

In Julia's office, Elaine cried as she talked about what she knew had to happen. She and Phil would have to sell their house and move somewhere else, probably an independent living apartment in a continuing care retirement community (CCRC), which provides levels of care should they ever need it. Elaine had begun to recognize that their life was going to change in a big and permanent way. She felt overwhelmed and alone. Julia and Elaine decided the next step would be to get Phil in for a joint appointment.

Despite the emotional challenges, we encourage couples we counsel to look at downsizing and moving as opportunities for positive change, a new beginning, a chance to meet new people and have new adventures. And the payoff? For all their trepidation, most couples we work with report increased satisfaction once they've made the move and settled into their new place. In our experience, we've found that couples can accomplish this by making the decision jointly, aligning their goals and wishes, and creating a dream home together.

Making a Joint Decision

The decision to downsize and move can feel overwhelming and typically comes with uncertainty due to a host of issues, emotional and practical. We help clients walk through the feelings and talk together about why they want to move—and why they don't. What are they sad about losing? What are they scared about? With all the clearing out to be done and factors to consider in moving, it is wise for spouses to start discussing their thoughts and feelings long before they must decide. If couples can take their time, explore what is important to each of them, listen to each other's hopes and wishes, and work within reality-based limitations, they will feel much less stress as they go through the process. But these conversations can be especially difficult if one partner wants to move and the other digs in his heels to stay. Weighing the pros and cons together takes time to allow for reflection and debate. Coming together around a cooperative plan can take weeks, months, and, for a few of our clients, years.

By the time Phil and Elaine came for their joint appointment, a medical change had forced a decision. Going up to his office, Phil had missed a step, lost his balance, and fallen down the stairs, fracturing his right arm. Phil finally admitted it was time for them to move. In Julia's office, they began to discuss what to do and where to go. Elaine brought up as many options as she could imagine. As they explored their future, even Phil began to consider the possibilities and make some suggestions himself.

Aligning Goals and Wishes

When couples finally decide to downsize and move, they must choose where to go. Are they clear on their priorities? Should their next home be an apartment, a smaller house, or a townhome? Single story? In an over-fifty-five community with a clubhouse and golf course? Or do they need some assistance? How much? What is their price range? Do they need space or nearby hotels for visiting family? A walkable town center? Quiet places to contemplate nature? Nearby current healthcare providers—or will couples have to find new ones?

A couple that Barry counseled couldn't agree on where they'd move after they sold their suburban home. They debated and argued until the wife suggested they buy a recreational vehicle and spend several months visiting the places they were considering. Although the husband was reluctant, he agreed to it. Several months turned into a year, and their search turned into a great adventure and brought them closer together than ever before. When they finally chose a place, they continued to take long trips each year in their RV.

A key point for Elaine and Phil: Where should they live? Elaine preferred staying close to friends and to Hope and her kids, who Elaine loved to visit. Phil wanted to move closer to their son, Rob, and his wife and two young kids, who lived where the weather was warmer and the cost of living was lower. Elaine was also thinking ahead, considering care they might need in the future. Their house was paid off, so they could sell and afford a CCRC, with everything on one level, some meals provided, and no home maintenance. That way, they wouldn't be a burden on their family. Phil agreed that a CCRC might be a good option. Many resources can help you decide where to move, including AARP's book *Wise Moves: Checklist for Where to Live, What to Consider, and Whether to Stay or Go,* by Sally Hurme and Lawrence Frolik.

Before they moved, they'd have to clear out a lot of stuff from their house. Downsizing is especially difficult when items have sentimental value. Some couples find that it's the perfect time to give extended-family members some of their valuable or treasured possessions as well as whatever else they may be able to use, as long as they agree to it. That can feel better than selling items, donating them, or dumping them in the trash. For valuable items that no one in the family wants, investigate antique or art auctions, suggests Marni Jameson, author of AARP's *Downsizing the Family Home: What to Save, What to Let Go*. Donate items no one wants to a charity you believe in.

Elaine and Phil found themselves bickering over what to keep, what to sell, and what to give away. Phil was attached to the living room furniture and wanted to replicate the comfort he felt in their current home. Elaine wanted to start fresh in a new home. Now that they were discussing the details, they realized how important it was to talk it all through.

We've found that downsizing and relocating can be an opportunity for couples to share what's most important and meaningful to each of them. Often, after years in one place, partners can take for granted that they have the same vision for what's next. As comfortable as they've been in their environment, it's important to take the time to explore new possibilities, think through what the future may look like, discuss the challenges that may arise as time passes, and make sure that they can reach compromises on their goals and wishes.

Between getting the house ready to be sold, caring for Phil's broken arm, and anticipating and trying to plan for the major changes that were about to occur in her life, Elaine felt exhausted. She shared her feelings of anxiety with Phil, who was empathic and spoke of his own concerns, worries, and sadness.

And there will be sadness, even mourning. The grieving process can take several months, but having watched couples go through the process, we can assure you it will pass. Keep your connections to friends and family and talk to each other about your feelings.

As Elaine and Phil talked and planned, they both began to feel like moving could be a good thing. And they felt closer as they shared their fears and hopes with each other.

They decided to visit several retirement communities, near both their current home and their son's. Elaine found herself getting excited about the opportunities for socializing, learning, and participating in organized activities and going on trips to museums and the theater. Quite a few people at each place welcomed them warmly. She felt reassured by the continuous care offered, if either of them ever needed it. And she was getting used to the idea of a warmer climate and proximity to their son and his family.

But Phil, though he'd accepted that they'd have to move and said the places all seemed nice, was overcome by grief. As he shared his feelings with Elaine, she could feel the sadness too. They'd had a glorious life in their home together. They would have to leave it all behind. It took her breath away. Could they build a new life together that would also be good for them? They spoke frequently about what life could be like in the new place. They'd have each other no matter where they were.

In the end, they decided to move near their son, as Phil preferred. Elaine felt it would make his transition easier. They found a place that had plenty of lectures and classes on-site, organized card games, transportation, jewelry making, a recreation room with a big-screen TV for watching sports, and a terrific state-of-the-art gym. They agreed that at least a few times a year, they'd come back to visit Hope or pay for her and the kids to visit.

Right before they moved out, they threw a big goodbye dance party with all their family and friends. It was a blast, with dancing late into the night and Elaine's closest friends helping to clean up afterward, all of them a bit teary. It was the perfect send-off.

Creating a Dream Home Together

Rob met them at the airport. Their furniture had arrived the day before. They piled into the car and headed away from the airport toward their new life.

As Elaine reported to Julia in a phone session, when they entered their new apartment, they were both shocked at how compact it seemed with all the furniture placed. Sure, they knew they were downsizing from a four-bedroom to a two-bedroom. But it was a tight fit. Phil's office furniture was stuffed into the second bedroom, with barely space to move. They had known there was no dining room—they'd be eating most dinners in the CCRC's dining room—but the kitchen was so tiny, with just enough room for a small table. They looked at each other. Had they made a big mistake? Could they adjust to a smaller home? They sat down on the couch in the small living room and looked around silently.

As Julia coached them on the phone session, adjusting to the transition to a new home can take at least several months and often up to half a year. Couples should try to be patient and mindfully focus on the positives. Decorating the new home in ways that bring joy is one way to aid the adjustment. Remembering to support each other through new social settings and interactions will ease the transition. Couples should get involved in the new community, beginning with a few activities or volunteer opportunities.

As most of our clients soon find out, the benefits to downsizing are enormous. A smaller house means less housework, and some communities provide housekeeping services and even laundry services. Couples who no longer own a home are relieved of home maintenance, long driveways to shovel, and lawns to mow. And because couples will have whittled down belongings to a manageable amount, they'll have less clutter and a more orderly, compact environment that can bring a sense of calm. Those moving into communities often have a range of activities, transportation, and a built-in social network outside their doors.

On their first night in their new home together, Elaine and Phil cuddled on the couch under a blanket, drinking sparkling cider from champagne glasses and discussing where to put the cherished pieces of art they'd kept. They would explore the community together in the morning.

Tying It All Together

Elaine ultimately found herself feeling upbeat and optimistic. She eagerly met new people and made friends easily. She was already a regular at the gym and joined the walking group. She'd be okay. And Phil was adjusting to their new environment, though more slowly, sometimes choosing the communal TV rather than their own and recognizing several other sports fans at dinner. Should they eventually need help, it would be available. And they were seeing Rob and his family much more frequently than they had. Elaine knew they would have struggles ahead. But together they would have the support of their family and the new community in which they'd soon feel at home.

How to Address Your Downsizing and Relocating Concerns

If you and your partner are considering downsizing and moving, or are in the process of doing so, consider taking the following Check-Up.

You and your partner should fill out the Check-Up separately and then compare your results. There are no right or wrong answers, only places where you and your partner may have diverging or similar feelings, experiences, or needs. All are important to know about. The divergent places are opportunities to share and learn so that you can plan mindfully how you'd like to handle downsizing and relocating.

DOWNSIZING AND RELOCATING CHECK-UP

1. My partner and I are both fully involved in making decisions about downsizing and moving.

   Strongly Disagree   Disagree   Neutral   Agree   Strongly Agree

2. My partner and I have planned to downsize and move at the best time for both of us.

   Strongly Disagree   Disagree   Neutral   Agree   Strongly Agree

3. My partner and I have taken the location of family into account.

   Strongly Disagree   Disagree   Neutral   Agree   Strongly Agree

4. My partner and I have taken the location of friends into account.

   Strongly Disagree   Disagree   Neutral   Agree   Strongly Agree

5. My partner and I have discussed where we want to move.

   Strongly Disagree   Disagree   Neutral   Agree   Strongly Agree

6. My partner and I have discussed the kind of home we want to move to.

   Strongly Disagree   Disagree   Neutral   Agree   Strongly Agree

7. My partner and I agree about housing extended family who visit.

   Strongly Disagree   Disagree   Neutral   Agree   Strongly Agree

8. My partner and I agree on the leisure activities we want to have around us.

   Strongly Disagree   Disagree   Neutral   Agree   Strongly Agree

9. My partner and I agree about financing the housing we'd like to move to.

   Strongly Disagree   Disagree   Neutral   Agree   Strongly Agree

10. My partner and I have spent time where we are planning to move to make sure it's a good fit.

    Strongly Disagree   Disagree   Neutral   Agree   Strongly Agree

11. My partner and I have imagined together what our lives will be like in the future.

    Strongly Disagree   Disagree   Neutral   Agree   Strongly Agree

12. My partner and I agree on the items in our home we will get rid of.

    Strongly Disagree   Disagree   Neutral   Agree   Strongly Agree

13. My partner and I agree on the items we want to keep.

    Strongly Disagree   Disagree   Neutral   Agree   Strongly Agree

14. My partner and I have been reducing our possessions in anticipation of the move.

    Strongly Disagree   Disagree   Neutral   Agree   Strongly Agree

15. My partner and I are using the downsizing process to remember meaningful occasions.

    Strongly Disagree   Disagree   Neutral   Agree   Strongly Agree

16. My partner and I feel like a team with regard to downsizing and moving.

    Strongly Disagree   Disagree   Neutral   Agree   Strongly Agree

17. My partner and I are excited about the possibilities of moving to a new place.

    Strongly Disagree   Disagree   Neutral   Agree   Strongly Agree

18. My partner and I agree about how we want to decorate our new space.

    Strongly Disagree   Disagree   Neutral   Agree   Strongly Agree

19. My partner and I talk about our feelings about leaving our home.

    Strongly Disagree   Disagree   Neutral   Agree   Strongly Agree

20. My partner and I support each other through feelings of grief.

    Strongly Disagree   Disagree   Neutral   Agree   Strongly Agree

Reviewing the Downsizing and Relocating Check-Up

If you differ by two or more degrees on 1, 2, 11, 15, 19, and 20: Make some time to discuss what you want to do about downsizing, when you want to do it, and how you feel about it.

If you differ on 3, 4, 5, and 16: Have a focused conversation about where you'd like to live, taking important issues like proximity to family and friends into account. Explore what situation will work best for both of you currently and in the future.

If you differ on 12, 13, and 14: You'll need to discuss what you want to hold on to and let go of as you downsize. Make use of resources such as AARP's *Downsizing the Family Home: What to Save, What to Let Go*. Often, getting expert advice can make this process easier.

If you differ on 6, 7, 8, or 9: Take some time to talk about the details of what you are looking for in your next home. Resources such as AARP's *Wise Moves* can help. Be as open and honest about your needs and wishes as you can so that you have the best chance of making a decision that works for both of you.

Next Steps

If you want to try to improve your emotional connection and develop a more shared vision as you go through the downsizing and moving transition, as well as increase your ability to cooperate and negotiate to meet the needs of both of you, here's what we suggest:

First, listen to each other at length; you can problem-solve together later. The process may feel slow and labored, but try to be patient with it; this will give you the best opportunity to fully know what your partner is thinking and feeling, and your partner will learn what you are thinking and feeling. This is an opportunity to get to know each other deeply regarding this major life transition. If you both agree to take your time with it, you will get the most from it.

Make an appointment to sit down together for an hour. You won't be making big decisions; you'll be sharing your Check-Up results and talking about where you agree and disagree. Take turns telling each other how you feel about downsizing and relocating, what the change means to you, the fears about potential loneliness or isolation, or the grief about the losses you may feel. Use the "Tips for Talking and Listening" found at the beginning of this book.

Let yourselves be vulnerable. Do your best to listen patiently, quietly, and nonjudgmentally. Give your partner time to talk. Remember that this isn't easy for either of you.

Respond to your partner with a validating comment, even if you feel surprised or upset. Just listen closely and summarize what your partner said, so you both feel heard. Be respectful and supportive. You aren't solving problems now; you are sharing feelings and learning about each other.

Remember that your goal is to feel more connected. End the hour by identifying areas of agreement from the Check-Up and setting a positive goal, such as beginning to clear out a room in your home, choosing the artwork you can't live without, or making an appointment to look at places you may like to move to. This will be an opportunity to feel closer.

A Week Later

Because your feelings about your home and your future have developed over years, you'll need more time to review the Check-Up and discuss areas of agreement and disagreement. The goal is to work toward a mutually acceptable compromise in which both of you feel heard and supported.

About a week after you discuss your Check-Up results, meet again to share any additional reactions to your findings and begin formulating a plan for downsizing and relocation.

Here are some questions to spur your conversation:

- How do each of you feel about moving out of your home? What meaning does it have for you?
- What is your plan of action for decluttering your home?
- Is it financially wise to downsize?
- Would buying or renting a new home or moving into a community for older adults make more sense?
- How do you each feel about being near family and friends?
- Are there choices that would bring more happiness as you consider where to move, such as access to nature, good weather, or cultural activities?
- Will you want to have space for large dinners and visiting guests in your new home, or would it make better financial sense to rent out a party room or have guests stay in a nearby hotel?
- How will you engage in your new community together?
- What do each of you want and need from your new community?
- What do each of you want and need from each other?
- Can you negotiate your needs in a thoughtful, caring, cooperative way so that you both feel satisfied?

An Ongoing Plan to Integrate Change

All plans need regular review and refinement to remain fresh, relevant, and effective. Meet again at least monthly to talk about how you are both feeling and continue to plan your future together. Make time to talk about what you need and how you might assist each other. As you continue to negotiate compromise, keep in mind the implications of the decisions you are making. What personal sacrifices can you tolerate making? The more concrete and detailed you can be in your conversations, the less likely you are to encounter misunderstanding and disagreement later.

Share your reflections about downsizing and relocation. You won't likely agree in full about everything, but you should be accepting and respectful as you continue to search for workable compromises. Your goal is to nurture your relationship by demonstrating your care for each other as you face these new challenges together. Even as you continue to work on the myriad details of downsizing and relocation, try to share feelings, remember shared experiences, and support each other.

Steps to Success

Downsizing and relocating can be a tough transition for couples to manage. Stepping up to the challenge together gives you the best chance of making the most of the opportunity to start fresh and feel good about your future. We recommend the following:

- Talk through the pros and cons as you work to make decisions together. The goal is to make choices that are acceptable to both of you.
- Take your time to work out the when, where, and how of moving, making sure that your goals and wishes for the future are aligned.

- Recognize that both of you have emotional reactions to these big changes in your lives. Share them with each other.

- Continue to try to understand and empathize with the other's point of view.

- Spend time together to thoughtfully make choices that take the needs and wishes of both of you into account.

- Work to create a dream home together.

- Consult a professional if you struggle to make a plan that is mutually acceptable.

To proceed successfully through this transition, you should have approximately the same vision and agree about what features are important. You are planning the next stage of your journey together. This means taking your time and expressing your wishes as well as listening carefully to your partner's wishes. Make sure you have talked it all through, reached compromises where necessary, and supported each other emotionally as you've moved through the process. Many people feel excited about this transition, but it can also bring up feelings of fear and loss.

Work together as a team to prepare to move and to make the important decisions about when and where you'll move to. Keep in mind what each of you wants and needs and try to support each other through the process. Your goal is to feel more connected. Try to be patient as you discuss your concerns, needs, and wishes for the future. Downsizing is difficult. Relocating can feel like a loss, even in the best of circumstances. Show compassion for each other. Even if you continue to work on areas in which you disagree, try to share feelings, remember shared experiences, grieve together, and aim for compromise and good boundaries.

Once you have relocated, be sure to be a team about acclimating to your new environment. Take walks together, make new friends and introduce them to your partner, and share what you have explored and learned. Keep talking about your feelings, fears, and joys. Recognize that this big transition is stressful and reassure each other that you are there, going through this new adventure together.

Challenge 7

Sex

"We've gone on romantic dates like you suggested," Carol told Julia at their counseling session. "Fancy candlelit dinners. They've been fun. And then we come home and I shut down."

"You mean sexually?" Julia asked.

Carol nodded: "I just don't feel it. I can't go further."

"I know she needs time," Ben said. "But I'm not sure what to do."

For many couples as they age, sex can become more challenging for emotional and physical reasons. For Ben and Carol, past infidelities and years of emotional distance had taken a toll. Old hurts, conflict, physical changes, stress and anxiety, low self-esteem, busy lifestyles, loss of loved ones: These and more can all find their way into the bedroom. Some couples neglect to maintain their sense of playfulness because they'd spent years focused on work or children.

For most couples, though, sex matters. Nearly 60 percent of people over fifty believe sex is a critical part of a good relationship, according to "Sex, Romance, and Relationships: AARP Survey of Midlife and Older Adults." Its absence can contribute to a lack of emotional closeness in couples, and vice versa.

Sometimes sexual challenges can be attributed to a medical issue. According to the AARP survey, close to one in four men (23 percent) say they have been diagnosed with erectile dysfunction or impotence. Whenever a couple comes to therapy with a sexual problem, we start by recommending that both partners undergo a medical evaluation. Sometimes the solution is as simple as a prescription for erectile dysfunction or an over-the-counter lubricant for dryness and discomfort. Sometimes, sexual dysfunction is a side effect of medication. But often enough, couples have ignored or avoided their sexual concerns long enough that they've developed barriers that can compound the difficulties of restoring an active sex life.

Barry worked with one couple whose wife admitted she often tried to avoid any affectionate behaviors—even hugging and handholding—lest her husband interpret them as an interest in sex. And she just wasn't interested. This across-the-board rejection of all physical contact exacerbated the couples' sense of disconnection. Plenty of other couples avoid sex because worries about body image or sexual functioning have led to self-consciousness and performance anxiety. Over the years, we've both worked with men who became so concerned that they won't be able to perform sexually that it led to a kind of self-fulfilling prophecy.

Couples who don't suffer these psychological complications still have to adjust to the physiological changes of aging. When they are doing well together, many claim that sex has become more enjoyable for them over the years. Everything slows down in a good way. Couples report more affection and spend more time hugging, kissing, touching, and enjoying time together. And those who have been together a long time frequently report feeling more relaxed and intimate than in their earlier years. They know each other well enough emotionally and physically to confidently communicate about and meet each other's needs.

This isn't surprising. We've worked with many clients to overcome the myriad increasing challenges to a healthy and more satisfying sex life, helping them to create an environment in which they feel safe and comfortable sharing their intimate concerns with each other. We encourage couples to work through three steps to get there: rekindling lost love, communicating without self-consciousness, and adjusting expectations.

Rekindling Lost Love

Mind and body work together, and it's therefore essential for couples to attend to their emotional relationship while trying to rekindle their physical one. In our clinical experience, increasing physical intimacy can often enhance emotional closeness, but the physical contact must be handled in a way to lower, not amplify, performance anxiety.

Julia recommended to Ben and Carol that they begin with the mindful reintroduction of nonsexual touch into their everyday lives.

"It's terrific that you are enjoying going on dates and kissing, but it sounds like you need to take it up a notch," Julia said. "How do you feel about welcoming each other home with a kiss and a hug after work? Giving each other massages? Cuddling under a blanket together to watch a movie? I'm sure you can come up with a lot of ways to be more physically attentive and playful with touch without heading directly to the bedroom." These were all ways of showing affection that Ben and Carol had naturally gravitated to early on in their relationship but had forgotten about in more recent years.

Or maybe they hadn't forgotten—just neglected. Like many couples, they'd worked stressful jobs and raised children, inadvertently putting their everyday intimate relationship on a back burner. But that, in turn, led to discomfort with closeness, lack of communication, avoidance, and, in the case of Ben and Carol, betrayals. They'd no longer felt comfortable being vulnerable with each other. Regaining that comfort would be a crucial piece of rebuilding their trust and intimacy. When partners can be vulnerable with each other and sensitively respect each other in that vulnerability, then old wounds can be healed and partners can feel more confident in each other and in themselves—and less tense around each other physically.

Aside from stimulating sexual interest, touch, including hugging, hand-holding, and massage, can reduce stress hormones and increase the release of calming hormones. Physical touch has been found to be reassuring, comforting, and relaxing. It generally increases positive feelings between people. As long as both partners are agreeable to it, caring physical touch enhances relationships at all levels.

Maintaining a loving intimate relationship requires mindful and joyful effort on a regular basis. This includes a variety of types of physical touch as well as plenty of affectionate communication. Simple expressions matter. According to a survey of more than eight thousand people, among the happiest couples, 85 percent say "I love you" and 74 percent kiss passionately at least once a week.

Feeling close to each other is the most important feature of the relationship. "Friendship is the glue that can hold a marriage together," says John Gottman, a world-renowned psychological researcher on marriage. It makes sense that when couples know each other well— their likes, dislikes, wishes, and fantasies—they are happier together emotionally and sexually.

Barry McCarthy, a psychologist and expert on aging and sexuality, describes five types of touch: affectionate, sensual, playful, erotic, and intercourse. He suggests that keeping them all in mind and engaging in them in sequence helps couples become more aware of each other's preferences and slows down the approach to sex, making it more likely to be satisfying for both partners.

So Ben and Carol left with a clear homework assignment: Continue connecting on an emotional level. Sprinkle in more touch.

Communicating Without Self-Consciousness

In their next appointment with Julia, Ben and Carol both reported that the physical playfulness felt a little forced at first, but then they both began to enjoy it. It did make them feel more connected to each other. As the weeks passed, they began to expect it and it became a more natural part of their interactions. They gave each other back massages after the gym one evening. They found a romantic movie and cuddled up under a blanket to watch it together. They took Julia's suggestion and became more physically playful whenever they saw an opportunity.

On one occasion, they found their way into the bedroom and thought they might try to engage sexually. But Carol continued to feel shut down and Ben couldn't maintain an erection. They hugged and kissed and gave up.

"Well, we tried," Carol said to Julia, and the couple laughed.

For many couples, feeling connected isn't enough to rekindle their intimacy. As they age, people frequently struggle with self-consciousness about their bodies and how they function. It was clear to Julia that Ben and Carol were struggling with these concerns. Women in particular can become increasingly judgmental about their physical appearance: weight gain, wrinkles, poor muscle tone. It's hard to feel sexy and comfortable in the bedroom with those self-critical attitudes. Or they may lose bladder control or experience painful vaginal dryness, which may make it easier just to avoid sex.

Vaginal dryness is a typical change that comes with aging, which can make intercourse uncomfortable and even painful. New products are coming out regularly, including hormone creams and high-tech vaginal lubricants.

Sexual dysfunction in men increases with age and is generally caused by decreased sexual desire, decreased ability to have and maintain an erection, and decreased ability to have an orgasm. Medications for hypertension, heart disease, diabetes, or stroke can increase the rate of sexual dysfunction. For men over fifty, about 26 percent struggle with some degree of erectile dysfunction; for those over seventy, that jumps to 61 percent. Lifestyle choices, like regular exercise and a healthy diet, can slow these changes down but aren't likely to prevent them altogether.

A man can feel such shame that he isn't willing to keep trying and then winds up avoiding sex altogether. That withdrawal can make his partner feel unattractive, rejected, frustrated, and possibly angry. If she starts to avoid sex as well and withdraws emotionally, then the couple has no opportunity to talk about and manage the erection failure. This, in turn, can lead to disaffection and alienation.

Medications like Viagra can address the problem. They can increase blood flow to the penis, thereby improving male sexual functioning.

For both men and women, we've found that the solution is not just pills and creams—even when those work. More bodily touch, longer foreplay, and less focus on intercourse and orgasm can bring couples closer and often leads to more satisfying lovemaking. Partners who understand how best to please each other and have developed improved sexual techniques may not mind the changes that come with aging.

Being self-conscious and embarrassed about bodily functions can upturn a couple's sexual relationship and deepen any emotional distance between them. Partners may steer clear of intimate interactions. Just talking about their concerns about physical changes is a challenge. They may also feel constrained about talking openly about how their sexual feelings and needs have changed. Even more challenging is discussing how they would like to relate to each other sexually given these changes. Professionals can help, but some couples don't think of reaching out to them or feel too ashamed to do so.

Closing relationship gaps requires understanding of what's going on, lots of communication, and mutual tolerance. Partners should focus their attention on attending to each other and giving each other pleasure while not evaluating their own appearance. Studies have found that as people age, they actually tend to be more likely to find their partners physically attractive.

Since Ben and Carol hadn't had sex with each other for several years, Julia thought it might be possible that they had gone through some physical changes in the interim. She asked if they'd discussed this. They both shook their heads. Their self-consciousness, Julia explained, had gotten in the way of their talking about what each of them preferred or needed sexually. Bodies change as people age—nothing to be embarrassed about. They could discuss the changes they were experiencing. She talked about how physiological response time is slower for both men and women and that there is often more need for foreplay. This can be a positive factor in the relationship, an opportunity to take the time to relax and enjoy each other. She asked them to try to talk about what each of them wants, to listen closely, and to use their conversations as a guide to improving their enjoyment of physical closeness. Meanwhile, they'd continue with the increased physical contact, whether it led to sex or not. Julia ended the session by recommending that Ben see a doctor to determine the cause of his erectile dysfunction. Carol agreed to purchase a lubricant.

Adjusting Expectations

The bottom line, Carol and Ben were learning, was that sex wouldn't look or even feel the same as it had twenty years ago. The challenge was to be creative, flexible, and accepting—to change their expectations.

Could they comfortably talk about their experiences and wishes? Could they expand their views of sexual behaviors and adapt their sexual practices to account for physical changes? Could they derive closeness and gratification from a slightly different kind of sex life?

Here are some suggestions for sex after fifty that Julia shared with Carol and Ben:

1. Change the time of day that you engage in sex. You'll feel like you're sneaking away!
2. Move sex out of the bed and even out of the bedroom.
3. Try some new positions. (That's also important if you're having some achy body parts that you want to avoid.)
4. Use pillows creatively.
5. Arrange for a romantic atmosphere: candles, lingerie, a quiet dinner for two.
6. Shower or bathe together.
7. Keep the lubrication handy.
8. Don't stress the need for intercourse. You don't need a goal.
9. And you don't need to hurry. Take more time. The mechanics may take longer—and the feelings can be savored for longer.
10. Turn off the devices.

Whatever you do, Julia counseled them, talk together about what works and what doesn't as you explore ways to improve your sex life.

Barry McCarthy, an expert on aging and sexuality, recommends that couples aim for good-enough sex. He views sex as a positive part of a relationship that provides satisfaction, pleasure, comfort, and intimacy. Couples should approach it realistically and with knowledge of normal changes in biology, psychology, and relationships. Staying in good physical health, maintaining healthy habits together, and making time for relaxation all support sexual health. "Desire and satisfaction are more important than arousal and orgasm," McCarthy says. "Valuing variable, flexible couple sexual experiences and abandoning the 'need' for perfect individual sex performance inoculates you against sexual dysfunction by reducing performance pressure, fear of failure, and partner rejection." He views sexuality as "playful, energizing, spiritual, and special."

As Ben and Carol discussed with Julia their worries about the challenges in their sexual relationship, they began to relax. Normalizing the discussion of sexual concerns allowed them to view it as pretty much like any other topic. There were facts to be learned, adjustments to be made, and ways to care for each other better. It was all in the service of improving their marriage.

Tying It All Together

Ben and Carol returned to meet with Julia after several weeks. Ben's doctor had switched his blood pressure medicine to see if that helped. When it didn't, Ben made another appointment and Carol had gone with him for support. The doctor prescribed a medication for erectile dysfunction and referred Ben to a urologist for further evaluation.

They'd given the medication a try along with lots of foreplay and patience, some lubrication, and moments of nervous laughter. They had found that even after several years of absence, they could enjoy sexual intimacy again. It wasn't exactly the smooth sailing it had been years before, but it felt more intimate and sweeter. They were on their way to regaining their sex life but in a new and improved, more meaningful way. And along the way, they'd learned that there are many ways to have sexual intimacy, even when all the parts don't work as well as they used to. Sex could once again enhance their marriage.

How to Address Your Sexual Concerns

If you and your partner have concerns about your sexual functioning and feel that it could use some improvement, consider taking the following Check-Up.

You and your partner should fill out the Check-Up separately and then compare your results. There are no right or wrong answers, only places where you and your partner may have diverging or similar feelings, experiences, or needs. All are important to know about. The divergent places are opportunities to share and learn so that you can plan mindfully how you'd like to improve your sex life.

SEXUAL CONCERNS CHECK-UP

1. My partner and I discuss our sexual wishes with each other.

   Strongly Disagree   Disagree   Neutral   Agree   Strongly Agree

2. My partner and I have maintained feelings of passion for each other.

   Strongly Disagree   Disagree   Neutral   Agree   Strongly Agree

3. My partner and I plan romantic activities on a regular basis.

   Strongly Disagree   Disagree   Neutral   Agree   Strongly Agree

4. My partner and I have spoken to our family physicians about changes in our sexual experiences.

   Strongly Disagree   Disagree   Neutral   Agree   Strongly Agree

5. My partner and I have tried or would try lubricants or medications to help improve our sex life.

   Strongly Disagree   Disagree   Neutral   Agree   Strongly Agree

6. My partner and I cuddle and it doesn't always lead to sex.

   Strongly Disagree   Disagree   Neutral   Agree   Strongly Agree

7. My partner and I have been flexible about making changes in our sex life to accommodate changing needs.

   Strongly Disagree   Disagree   Neutral   Agree   Strongly Agree

8. My partner and I show affection and appreciation to each other regularly.

   Strongly Disagree   Disagree   Neutral   Agree   Strongly Agree

9. My partner and I would consider seeing a psychotherapist or other professional for sexual issues.

   Strongly Disagree   Disagree   Neutral   Agree   Strongly Agree

10. My partner and I are comfortable with each other's fluctuations in sexual desire.

    Strongly Disagree   Disagree   Neutral   Agree   Strongly Agree

11. My partner and I recognize how stress can impact our sex life.

Strongly Disagree   Disagree   Neutral   Agree   Strongly Agree

12. My partner and I try to reduce stress and our reactions to it as much as we can.

Strongly Disagree   Disagree   Neutral   Agree   Strongly Agree

13. My partner and I recognize that masturbation is part of normal sexuality.

Strongly Disagree   Disagree   Neutral   Agree   Strongly Agree

14. My partner and I say sexy things to each other just for the fun of it.

Strongly Disagree   Disagree   Neutral   Agree   Strongly Agree

15. My partner and I agree that drinking or drug use can impact our sex life.

Strongly Disagree   Disagree   Neutral   Agree   Strongly Agree

16. My partner and I know that staying healthy impacts our sex life and try to take care of ourselves.

Strongly Disagree   Disagree   Neutral   Agree   Strongly Agree

17. My partner and I have worked out past affairs or conflicts and feel at peace with them.

Strongly Disagree   Disagree   Neutral   Agree   Strongly Agree

18. My partner and I are patient with each other while engaging in sexual behaviors.

Strongly Disagree   Disagree   Neutral   Agree   Strongly Agree

19. My partner and I take precautions when necessary with regard to sexually transmitted diseases.

Strongly Disagree   Disagree   Neutral   Agree   Strongly Agree

20. My partner and I plan to continue having a sex life for as long as possible.

Strongly Disagree   Disagree   Neutral   Agree   Strongly Agree

Reviewing the Sexual Concerns Check-Up

Try to be open, accepting, and nonjudgmental about what you learn about each other. Your purpose is to improve your sexual relationship, but that can take time. Talking about sex can be a delicate process. Try to be patient and supportive and remember that you aren't going to quickly solve anything that has developed over time.

If you have three or more widely diverging answers (on opposite sides of the "neutral" choice): You and your partner likely aren't entirely happy with your current sex life. You probably need to address your sexual issues.

If you diverge on numbers 1, 4, 5, 7, and 9: You probably aren't talking to each other or a professional about your feelings and how the changes in your sex life are affecting you. Shame can prevent people from facing their concerns and getting the help they need. Encourage each other to learn about the issues, speak to professionals, and normalize the experience.

If you don't agree on numbers 2, 3, 8, and 20: You probably need to talk about how important your sex life is to each of you. Are you having other relationship problems that are interfering with your comfort in the bedroom? Have you begun to take each other for granted? Do you both value sharing pleasure together? If these questions are difficult to answer, it may be time to consider couples counseling to strengthen your intimate bond. Sometimes these issues are difficult to address on your own.

Next Steps

If you want to try to improve your sexual intimacy and increase your ability to cooperate and negotiate to meet the needs of both of you, here's what we suggest:

Make an appointment to sit down together for an hour. You won't be making big decisions; you'll be sharing your Check-Up results and talking about where you agree and disagree. Take turns telling each other how you feel about the state of your sexual intimacy. Are some aspects satisfying? Are there ways in which your needs are not being met? Describe to the best of your ability what you feel you want and need. Would your partner be willing to try something new? Be kind, as it isn't so easy to discuss these issues and concerns. Use the "Tips for Talking and Listening" found at the beginning of this book.

Let yourselves be vulnerable. Do your best to listen patiently, quietly, and nonjudgmentally. Give your partner time to talk. Remember that this isn't easy for either of you.

Respond to your partner with validating comments, even if you feel surprised, upset, or defensive. Just listen closely and summarize what your partner said, so you both feel heard. Be respectful and supportive. You aren't solving problems now; you are sharing feelings and learning about each other.

Remember that your goal is to feel more connected. End the hour by identifying areas of agreement from the Check-Up and setting a positive goal, such as an intimate evening out, cuddling up in front of a movie together, or even trying something new. This will be an opportunity to feel closer.

A Week Later

Sexual intimacy is a sensitive, delicate topic. You are negotiating your sexual relationship in a nonthreatening and nonshaming way. You've learned something about each other already, and now you need to make a plan of action.

About a week after you discuss your Check-Up results, meet again to share any additional reactions to your findings and begin formulating a plan to improve your sexual relationship.

Here are some questions to spur your conversation:

- Would one or both of you benefit from seeing a doctor, and should you go together?
- Are you feeling shame or embarrassment? Can you move past these feelings to talk about your needs?
- Do you feel like a team working together in the process of improving your feelings of sexual intimacy?
- Are you both able to be patient and try new things?
- Are you both able to focus on pleasing and supporting each other?
- Do stress or self-esteem concerns get in the way of your enjoyment of sex?
- What can each of you do for the other to improve sexual experience?
- Are certain positions painful to one of you? What can you do differently?
- What do each of you want and need from each other?
- Can you negotiate your needs in a thoughtful, caring, cooperative way so that you both feel satisfied?

This is an opportunity to find new ways of caring for each other. Make a plan to spend time together engaged in an intimate activity exploring ways you can take care of each other that you both can enjoy. Share your feelings about it with each other afterward.

An Ongoing Plan to Integrate Change

Plan to meet again to talk about how you are both feeling now that you've spent time sharing your wishes about sexual intimacy. If you've made the effort, you will both find it easier to discuss your sexual issues and interests. You don't have to agree on what you prefer, but you should be accepting and respectful as you continue to work on your developing relationship. Your goal is to feel more connected emotionally and sexually and to be better able to value and care for each other. As you continue to address potentially challenging issues within your sex life, try to share feelings, remember shared experiences, confront shame, grieve together if necessary, and aim for closeness, trust, and care. A couple's intimate life can continue to be a valuable aspect of their relationship for many years ahead.

Steps to Success

To achieve a more positive sex life, plan to talk together about what you need, what works, and what isn't working. We recommend the following:

- Remember that many people feel self-conscious discussing their sex lives, so plan for a comfortable, private conversation. Try to communicate without self-consciousness.
- Listen carefully without judgment. Your goal is to talk about your needs and learn about your partner's needs.
- As time passes, continue to talk about your changing needs.
- Make an effort to set the stage for relaxation and romance.
- Do little thoughtful acts for each other.

- Focus on touching and being affectionate, even if it doesn't lead to sex.

- Face physical changes together as a team.

- Avoid discussing your worries when you are spending intimate time together.

- Even when you aren't being intimate, do something enjoyable together.

- Add in more foreplay and stay flexible.

Take your time. Discover new ways to be together. At this stage of the game, sex is about feeling close to each other and having a special, exciting, intimate relationship. That is one of the great joys of being part of a couple.

Challenge 8

Health Concerns

The research is clear. Being happily married is good for your health. Compared to those who are single or unhappily married, happily married people have fewer heart attacks and strokes. They survive surgeries more often, find cancer sooner with better outcomes, and live longer. They are less likely to struggle with mental health issues.

But none of us are immune forever to changes in our health. Sometimes these physical, emotional, or cognitive problems are relatively inconsequential and can be addressed by minor interventions or life-style changes: aches and pains, colds, weight gain or loss. Sometimes more serious changes have a long-term or complex impact on how an individual functions and spouses interact: acute or chronic phys-ical conditions, emotional difficulties, or cognitive decline. To cope, couples need to address these changes together, supporting each other in sickness and in health. The challenge is to remain a happy couple, making the most of the benefits demonstrated in the research, despite whatever changes may occur.

Elaine and Phil were struggling to do that. They had supported each other in their self-care efforts, eating well and going to the gym together for years, and enjoyed a mostly happy relationship. But after they had moved to a retirement community near their son, Rob, Elaine called Julia because she was concerned about Phil. Their adjustment to their new life had gone well in many respects. They enjoyed meals with new friends, lectures, classes, movies, and time with Rob and his family. At first, they'd gone on a few excursions to museums and malls. But lately, Phil had refused to join her whenever a trip was on the agenda because, Elaine suspected, of the physical toll: He struggled to stand or walk for long. The pain had gotten worse despite his knee replacements. Whether she left him at home or dragged him along, she felt guilty. When she tried to discuss her dilemma with him, he'd tell her he felt fine staying in the apartment and refused to address it.

Because it isn't often possible to predict when physical, emotional, or cognitive changes will occur, it is important for partners to mindfully strengthen their relationships and promote each other's well-being long before health concerns arise. That means encouraging each other to exercise, eat right, and have regular medical check-ups but also to shore up the marriage. Building reliability, trust, and affection over many years is like putting money in the bank to be drawn upon if and when illness strikes. That's the greatest assurance that partners will be there for each other when one becomes hard of hearing or short of breath climbing stairs and the other deals with diabetes, increased anxiety, or even cognitive decline.

For couples to best support each other with health concerns, we have found it's important to take the following steps: accept limitations, plan ahead, and take a team approach.

Accept Limitations

You may know people who refuse to get hearing aids or use canes, even though those assistive devices would improve their ability to enjoy socializing and getting around. They deny having problems at all but then avoid conversations, walks, and other activities that would expose their limitations. We've seen clients get angry at themselves or their partners when memories aren't as sharp or immune systems not as strong as they used to be. They feel ashamed and often prefer to cut themselves off rather than reveal a limitation or need. They are not only hurting themselves; they are hurting their relationships with their spouses.

As in the case of Phil. His walking was getting more unsteady, even without stairs to climb. He had worn out his knees playing basketball into his fifties and hadn't benefited much from the recent knee replacements. When Elaine suggested he use a cane, she wasn't surprised when he insisted that he didn't need one. She told Julia, in a private phone session, that she knew he'd be stubborn and proud to his own detriment.

Julia suggested that Elaine and Phil have a heart-to-heart talk about how they were doing since they'd moved into the retirement community. She suggested they ask each other about their moods and goals as well as how they could help each other. They needed to listen to each other and work to get back on the same team.

Many spouses have an unspoken understanding about the importance of self-care: Caring for their own health is a way they care for each other. This can mean facing physical, emotional, and cognitive health changes in themselves and making sometimes difficult choices to address them. Each expects the other to do what he can—whether that means going to the doctor for check-ups or when there's a problem, exercising, eating well, or using assistive devices, if necessary, to maintain his physical, emotional, and cognitive well-being. When one partner seems to neglect or even undermine his own health, the other can feel frustrated, hurt, and even betrayed. It's as if the neglectful spouse doesn't care that he may prevent them both from participating in activities, become a burden to his partner, or even shorten his life span.

We know of a woman who refused to visit a doctor for thirty years, despite her partner's prodding. Long-standing gastrointestinal issues led to her collapse, EMTs on the scene, and a diagnosis of abdominal cancer. She was dead in three months, leaving her partner alone and grieving, with financial and legal issues that took months to resolve.

When a couple has been together for years, it can be especially challenging for partners to acknowledge functional changes in each other. Often both partners deny the extent of the changes and the impact on their relationship. Typically, as time has passed, they've come to expect that they can rely on each other to manage certain responsibilities and chores. They don't want to see their partner in a vulnerable or weakened state, unable to keep up. For many people, it isn't easy to accept their own increasing limitations, not to mention the limitations of someone they love.

A couple with this issue came in to meet with Barry. The wife had had dementia for two years and was declining but still seemed quite capable. The husband left her alone all day while he drove a delivery truck, believing she was fine at home. When their daughter showed up to visit her mother one afternoon, she found that her mother had forgotten to eat or drink all day and was dizzy and unsteady. Barry worked with the couple to help the husband shift his views about his wife's needs and acknowledge the painful feelings of fear and loss behind his denial.

Spouses may need to face difficult changes in and even losses of physical, emotional, or cognitive health. When they acknowledge any limitations, they can more successfully move on to plan actions and find solutions, which in turn strengthens their connection and prevents their relationship from becoming unbalanced.

A good starting point is when the ill spouse is able to admit to limitations and fears about being a burden. Those feelings of shame often impede important conversations from occurring and breed feelings of neglect for both partners. They need to show each other that they care and that they'll both try to be there for each other in whatever ways they can be.

When Elaine and Phil sat down to have that heart-to-heart, Phil admitted his grief and frustration over his knee pain and physical limitations. Elaine offered to support him in whatever way she could, but Phil struggled to acknowledge that he needed her help at all. They'd need more conversations to work through his reluctance to make changes together, but at least they'd made a start.

Plan Ahead

A month later, Elaine reported to Julia that she felt hurt and frustrated that Phil didn't seem to be trying. He kept insisting that he just wanted to remain in the apartment. When she would return from an outing or a lecture, he seemed barely interested in hearing about it. When she stayed home with him, they often sat in silence. He didn't seem like himself. She felt rejected and lonely even when they were together, and she worried about him.

Julia recommended that Elaine and Phil have more conversations about how they could together enjoy their life and manage his knee pain. What activities could they still do together? What would make them both happy? What did Phil need to improve his enjoyment of life? What did they want their life to look like going forward? Focusing on his pain had left him sitting alone in their apartment, feeling it all the more. They needed to try a positive approach that focused on what Phil *could* do.

This team effort would apply not just to addressing Phil's knee pain but to managing both of their health changes as time passed. They needed to commit to caring for themselves and each other, and they needed to develop a strength-focused plan that would work for both of them. This would require continued open and honest communication about limitations and feelings and a willingness to make changes and possibly get help.

Generally, when we work with couples, we suggest that they begin these conversations as early as possible, before they face health challenges. We typically ask both partners in therapy how they want to manage physical, cognitive, and emotional health concerns. Do they want their partner to accompany them to medical appointments? Manage their partner's medications if necessary? Talk to the other partner's doctors? Do they like to do as much as they can before asking for help? Or is the first step seeking medical advice? What about end-of-life decisions, such as do-not-resuscitate orders? These conversations, approached with compassion, can help couples feel like a team addressing their potential and real challenges together over time.

One couple who met with Barry were surprised to learn that they had opposing views on medical choices. The husband felt strongly that if he were dying, he'd want his wife to do everything in her power to extend his life. The wife wanted no extreme measures taken for herself. They were glad to take the opportunity to talk through it so that they could be prepared to best care for each other.

For couples dealing with specific health issues, we encourage both partners to learn all they can together, get professional help when appropriate, and try to communicate about caregiving needs (see Challenge 9). Partners should try to imagine what the other is experiencing and may need from them. When Julia talked to Elaine again, she recommended that Elaine and Phil set up a meeting with the social worker on staff at their CCRC. When they did, she recommended a primary care provider for Phil to evaluate whether he needed to take an antidepressant and could refer him for physical therapy. Phil had never thought of himself as a depressed guy, even now when he was struggling with physical changes. He was surprised and a little offended to hear the social worker's appraisal. But it did make sense. As soon as they were back at their apartment, he called the doctor for an appointment.

Going to medical appointments together can be a way for couples to begin the sometimes-difficult conversations about health and to support each other. As couples come together to acknowledge and talk through their changing health and shifting needs, they can continue to thrive in their relationship. If they can find creative ways to work with new limitations and focus on their strengths, they can find a new balance together that will work into the future.

Take a Team Approach to Change

Planning alone isn't enough to bring about positive change. Couples need to make the commitment to work together to care for each other as they get older. The key to success is viewing the process as a team effort. When we talk to couples about supporting each other with a strength-based approach, we use a sports team metaphor because it includes all the necessary components. Effective teams address their challenges head-on, have a game plan, communicate well, connect emotionally, and include additional team members and supporters to ensure success.

This is demonstrated by the decades of research that have found a connection between having a strong social support network and positive health outcomes, including a 50 percent decreased risk of premature death. Spouses who believe that the best way to cope with shame-inducing physical or emotional challenges is to cut back on social activities may be putting their health at risk.

Fortunately, Elaine's new friends reached out to her, encouraging her to participate in the social activities she'd previously enjoyed. When she told them she was hesitant to leave Phil alone, one offered to stay with Phil while Elaine attended a lecture or class or took the grandchildren to the zoo. The neighbor showed up one day with two cups of coffee and spent hours chatting with Phil, who enjoyed her company. Another friend suggested that Phil sit in the sunroom adjacent to the jewelry-making class. Elaine designed jewelry while Phil basked in the warm sun and talked with people. These adjustments allowed both Elaine and Phil to feel more like part of the community and enjoy the company of others.

Rob and his family stepped in, too, when they could. Rob stopped by regularly on his way home for a few minutes, often bringing Phil a book to read or sitting with him to listen to music together. The grandkids did puzzles with him. Having family and friends helping them out gave them a feeling of comfort that they had a support system they could rely on.

Not everyone is as fortunate as Elaine and Phil. If you don't have a support network, consider starting to build one. It may feel awkward at first. Make time for family and friends. Reach out to others to ask for help with specific, small tasks. Neighbors may be happy to give you a ride or pick up a few items for you when they go to the grocery store. Ask younger family members to spend a little time helping out. Look into community resources around you and groups you can join to meet others in similar situations. Give to others so that when you ask for help, it feels reciprocal. You'll find a few people you can rely on, and who can rely on you.

Of course, you need to support each other first and foremost. Elaine and Phil needed to go back to functioning as a team. They needed to talk openly about what was happening and make a plan. Once he had been on an antidepressant for a few weeks, Phil realized he had felt so bad about himself that he'd neglected to think about Elaine's emotions at all. He had begun to feel better and was ready to now turn toward her again.

They sat down together and shared their feelings about the changes they had been going through. Elaine shared her fears, frustrations, and wishes. She missed their close connection, she told him. Phil had begun to realize he needed to actively take steps to care for Elaine. He missed their connection, too. He knew he'd been stubborn. He was making an effort to accept his physical limitations and use the walker more, and he always encouraged her to participate in whatever activities she wanted. To her relief, he was now trying.

After their conversation, Phil decided he would do even more. Elaine was thrilled when he announced he would begin physical therapy. He would do his best to build up his strength and learn how to get around better. Phil also agreed to participate in activities they could both enjoy. They decided to go to some of the lectures that were coming up as well as the movies that she'd been attending. They both looked forward to once again having the intellectually stimulating conversations they used to have.

When couples talk through their concerns, fears, and hopes and feel heard and validated, they can understand each other's needs more thoroughly and are more likely to support each other. If they can approach health as a team—working out together, eating healthy, understanding each other's limitations and care needs, planning for the future together, and bringing others in for support—then even when unexpected health concerns arise, they can face them together.

Tying It All Together

Several months later, Elaine told Julia that she and Phil felt like a team again, sharing activities that they could do together and enjoying time with friends and family. Phil went to physical therapy weekly and was steadier on his feet, and he had begun to join Elaine at the gym several times a week to do exercises to improve his walking. She was overjoyed that he had gotten past his shame and was making the effort to take care of himself and, by doing so, taking care of her. If they continued to band together to face and manage whatever health concerns came up, she felt confident they would have many happy years ahead.

How to Address Your Health Concerns

If you and your partner have health concerns and feel that your approach could use some improvement, consider taking the following Check-Up.

You and your partner should fill out the Check-Up separately and then compare your results. There are no right or wrong answers, only places where you and your partner may have diverging or similar feelings, experiences, or needs. All are important to know about. The divergent places are opportunities to share and learn so that you can plan mindfully how to handle physical, emotional, and cognitive health issues.

HEALTH CONCERNS CHECK-UP

1. My partner and I receive preventive medical care on a regular basis.

    Strongly Disagree   **Disagree**   **Neutral**   **Agree**   **Strongly Agree**

2. My partner and I share our medical information with each other.

    Strongly Disagree   **Disagree**   **Neutral**   **Agree**   **Strongly Agree**

3. My partner and I plan activities in which we can both participate.

    Strongly Disagree   **Disagree**   **Neutral**   **Agree**   **Strongly Agree**

4. My partner and I try to accommodate each other's physical, emotional, and cognitive limitations.

    Strongly Disagree   **Disagree**   **Neutral**   **Agree**   **Strongly Agree**

5. My partner and I try to support each other by taking care of ourselves.

    Strongly Disagree   **Disagree**   **Neutral**   **Agree**   **Strongly Agree**

6. My partner and I don't mind reminders about healthcare from each other.

    Strongly Disagree   **Disagree**   **Neutral**   **Agree**   **Strongly Agree**

7. My partner and I wouldn't ignore our physical health.

    Strongly Disagree   **Disagree**   **Neutral**   **Agree**   **Strongly Agree**

8. My partner and I try to make physical exercise enjoyable together and separately.

    Strongly Disagree   **Disagree**   **Neutral**   **Agree**   **Strongly Agree**

9. My partner and I support each other if we need help with emotional issues.

    Strongly Disagree   **Disagree**   **Neutral**   **Agree**   **Strongly Agree**

10. My partner and I talk about the health concerns that bother us. We don't bottle it up.

    Strongly Disagree   **Disagree**   **Neutral**   **Agree**   **Strongly Agree**

11. My partner and I stand by each other through emotionally challenging times.

    Strongly Disagree   Disagree   Neutral   Agree   Strongly Agree

12. My partner and I are there for each other through physical illness.

    Strongly Disagree   Disagree   Neutral   Agree   Strongly Agree

13. My partner and I get support from friends and family when managing emotional issues.

    Strongly Disagree   Disagree   Neutral   Agree   Strongly Agree

14. My partner and I get support from friends and family when dealing with physical challenges.

    Strongly Disagree   Disagree   Neutral   Agree   Strongly Agree

15. My partner and I trust that we will continue to support each other when one of us has a physical, emotional, or cognitive limitation.

    Strongly Disagree   Disagree   Neutral   Agree   Strongly Agree

16. My partner and I take care of ourselves to avoid or reduce physical, emotional, and cognitive issues.

    Strongly Disagree   Disagree   Neutral   Agree   Strongly Agree

17. My partner and I discuss our physical, emotional, or cognitive changes.

    Strongly Disagree   Disagree   Neutral   Agree   Strongly Agree

18. My partner and I make sure to have fun together in new ways if old ways don't work anymore.

    Strongly Disagree   Disagree   Neutral   Agree   Strongly Agree

19. My partner and I say yes when others offer assistance.

    Strongly Disagree   Disagree   Neutral   Agree   Strongly Agree

20. My partner and I agree that managing our health is a loving act.

    Strongly Disagree   Disagree   Neutral   Agree   Strongly Agree

Reviewing the Health Concerns Check-Up

If you have five or more widely diverging answers (on opposite sides of the "neutral" choice): You probably need to address your physical, emotional, and cognitive health issues.

If you diverge on numbers 1, 5, 8, 16, and 20: You probably don't see eye to eye about the value of self-care and how you can support each other. Try to understand each other's point of view by having conversations about your health. Then consider creating a plan that both of you can follow.

If you don't agree on numbers 2, 3, 6, 15, and 18: It may be time to sit down and take a hard look at how much you are willing to support each other and accept help when health issues arise. The goal is that both of you get your needs met. Committing to supporting each other to go to regular check-ups and follow an exercise routine would be a good starting point.

If you're far apart on numbers 9, 13, 14, or 19: You may want to discuss your willingness to accept support from others when in need and remember that having a supportive network of family and friends leads to better health outcomes.

Next Steps

If you want to try to improve your emotional connection as you care for each other with regard to your physical, emotional, and cognitive health, and increase your ability to cooperate and negotiate to meet the needs of both of you, here's what we suggest:

Make an appointment to sit down together for an hour. You won't be making big decisions; you'll be sharing your Check-Up results and talking about where you agree and disagree. Take turns telling each other how you feel about changes in physical, emotional, and cognitive health, whether actual or potential. Do you feel you can ask for what you need? Do you trust that your partner will be there for you? Have you made it clear that you will be supportive regarding changes in health? Use the "Tips for Talking and Listening" found at the beginning of this book.

Let yourselves be vulnerable. Do your best to listen patiently, quietly, and nonjudgmentally. Give your partner time to talk. Remember that this isn't easy for either of you.

Respond to your partner with validating comments, even if you feel surprised, defensive, or upset. Just listen closely and summarize what your partner said, so you both feel heard. Be respectful and supportive. You aren't solving problems now; you are sharing feelings and learning about each other.

Remember that your goal is to feel more connected and trusting about caring for yourselves and each other. End the hour by identifying areas of agreement from the Check-Up and setting a positive goal. Will you start a new exercise routine together? It could be as simple as a daily walk around the block. Do you want your partner to accompany you to your next medical appointment, join you in a counseling session, or see a nutritionist? Is there one thing that each of you can do to care for the other? This will be an opportunity to be more dedicated to focusing on your physical, emotional, and cognitive health as a couple and will help you to feel closer.

A Week Later

About a week after you discuss your Check-Up results, meet again to share any additional reactions to your findings and begin formulating a plan to deal with health concerns. You are negotiating to what extent you can rely on each other for your health needs and the degree to which caring for your and your partner's physical, emotional, and cognitive health is an important issue in your relationship. Taking care of your own health is a way to take care of your partner.

Here are some questions to spur your conversation:

- What can you do together that would improve your physical, emotional, or cognitive health?
- What would you like to change in your own healthcare habits?
- Do you need support from each other to reach healthcare goals?
- Do you prefer to involve extended family or friends when there is a health crisis for one of you?
- Do you both take responsibility for self-care and think of it as a way to care for each other?
- Are you satisfied with the way your partner takes care of his or her health?
- At what point do you both feel that bringing in outside hired help is acceptable?
- Are there ways that you could better support each other's emotional health?

Maintaining your health can make you feel like a team. Supporting each other through physical, emotional, and cognitive health challenges brings you closer as a couple, helps you understand each other better, and strengthens your bond. Find an activity you agree on that supports your health. It could be a regular conversation over coffee to discuss your emotional concerns. It could be a bike ride on a sunny weekend. Or you could develop a new meal plan together to adapt to changing dietary needs. Make a plan to spend time together engaged in something that you both feel supports physical, emotional, and cognitive health.

An Ongoing Plan to Integrate Change

Plan to meet again, and as many times as necessary, to talk about how you both feel about what you have learned about each other's needs regarding physical, emotional, and cognitive health. How do you both feel about the changes you are making as a couple to support your own health as well as your partner's? Discuss whether you each feel that your needs are being met. What are you still concerned about in yourself or your partner when it comes to your health? Are there issues that haven't been addressed? Do you each feel emotionally supported by the other? You don't have to agree on everything, but you should be accepting and respectful as you continue to work on your changing relationship.

Physical, emotional, and cognitive health continue to change as time goes by. You'll need to return to these conversations as new issues arise. Your goal is to feel more connected, trusting, and supportive toward yourself and each other regarding your physical, emotional, and cognitive health. Even as you continue to work on areas in which you disagree, try to share feelings, remember shared experiences, talk through differences, and aim for compromise and good boundaries.

Steps to Success

Your health is likely to change over time, so it is important to continue to communicate openly and flexibly about it. You should also discuss limits when it comes to providing care so that you can plan ways to bring in support.

Keep the following steps in mind as you go.

- Share feelings and concerns about changes in your health, even if you feel shame about what is happening to your body.

- Listen with acceptance and compassion.

- Acknowledge and address limitations together as they occur.

- Maintain an exercise schedule and a plan for healthy eating together.

- Plan activities together and pursue new experiences that accommodate changing needs.

- Negotiate time together and apart.

- Build a support network.

- Look for joy in everyday activities.

- Have conversations about the future.

- Make the most of your time together.

The goal is for both of you to feel that you are supporting each other as you do your best to maintain your health and manage any physical, emotional, or cognitive concerns that inevitably fall in your path. Whatever comes your way, you have each other to rely on and to turn to for care.

Caregiving

An estimated forty-one million people in the United States provide unpaid care to adults—whether spouses, parents, other relatives, or friends—according to "Valuing the Invaluable," a new AARP/National Alliance for Caregiving study. If you're reading about this challenge, you are likely one of the invaluable—or you will be soon.

We know the tremendous impact of caregiving from studies as well as from our clients and our own experiences. We cared for Julia's father and then Barry's mother and stepfather over a ten-year period. We've seen the tremendous toll caregiving takes on ourselves, our health, our finances, and our relationships. We've seen caregivers experience a roller coaster of difficult feelings: resentment, fear, sadness, and guilt.

This was true for James and Grace. After a long hiatus, they were back in Barry's office, once again sitting far apart and looking angry. Grace had had a few more small strokes, was less stable on her feet, and had begun dialysis three times a week for diabetes. James had retired several months earlier and had taken on more of the responsibilities: shopping, cleaning, taking Grace to her medical appointments, paying the bills, filling out the insurance forms. Rather than being grateful for his help, Grace complained that he wasn't doing the chores right, that he was buying the wrong items at the grocery store. He, in turn, felt resentful that he was doing all the work and wasn't appreciated.

James had other worries, too. His father, now in his late eighties, required more help than previously. James and his two brothers took turns shopping for their father and stopping by his apartment every day to straighten up and make sure he was eating and taking his medications. But James worried that his dad was still alone a lot. At the same time, he didn't like to leave Grace alone for long. Sometimes he felt like all he did nowadays was take care of other people.

According to "Caregiving in the United States," an AARP/National Alliance for Caregiving report, more than 40 percent of people providing unpaid care are adult children, and 12 percent are spouses. Nearly 20 percent, like James, are caring for more than one adult simultaneously.

Caregiving can significantly drive up your stress levels, put your health at risk, cut into savings, and eat up your free time and—for many—work time. It's not unusual for marital affection and intimacy to decrease. In our decades of meeting with caregivers and their spouses, we've found that by far the most challenging caregiving occurs when one spouse cares for the other. It almost always puts a multitude of stressors on the relationship.

Caring for aging parents, grown children, or other relatives or friends, however, brings different challenges. It can drive a wedge between partners if they don't agree on how much time, energy, and financial support they should provide. We've seen couples who have moved a parent into their home and then become consumed by caregiving duties, losing all semblance of normal married life. We've worked with couples where one partner resents how much time the other is spending on caregiving duties. In both scenarios, the spouses struggle with balancing marital needs with the obligation to ensure that everyone in the family is well cared for.

We've also seen partners care for a child with a chronic disability, such as cerebral palsy or an intellectual disability. Often, caregiving has been built into the fabric of that relationship over years, with the family dynamic centered on the needs of that child. But as the spouses and the child become older, a question looms: Will a day come when the child lives on his own with family and professional supports and the spouses turn their focus to their own relationship? Spouses sometimes disagree about what is the best choice for their child and themselves and are at odds for years.

The one message we'd like you to glean from this challenge is what we've learned from long experience: Caregiving is difficult. It is about sacrifice and responsibility and, more often than not (and no matter how much you're doing), guilt. But it is also a way to demonstrate love and enhance your sense of meaning and purpose in life. It can even bring great joy if partners communicate well and respect and support each other. In fact, research and our personal and professional experience show that caring for spouses or other loved ones can be truly meaningful and rewarding. It's gratifying for caregivers to know that they are making a significant difference. They may experience personal or spiritual growth and increased resilience through their commitment and sacrifices. They may feel like they are giving back to someone who cared for them, upholding their own moral or religious values, or even making up for hurtful mistakes in the past. Caregivers can enhance their sense of well-being and quality of life through the opportunity to take care of someone they love and have shared a life with for many years.

You can make the caregiving journey a positive and rewarding experience by pulling together, not apart; grieving the loss of loved ones and the loss of intimacy; and restoring joy.

Pulling Together, Not Apart

It would have been ideal for James and Grace to stand shoulder to shoulder against a common enemy—her illness and the way it was affecting their lives together, and the decline of James's father. Instead, to avoid what felt like overwhelming challenges, they bickered over the brand of cereal he bought and whether he vacuumed the corners. That was why they were still sitting at opposite sides of the couch.

In our experience, the main emotion that caregiving couples try to avoid is sadness—about the changes that have already occurred and the losses to come—as if feeling sad would be like a punch in the gut, deflating and debilitating them. But the ability to commiserate with each other is one of the most important ways partners can pull together in any adversity, including dealing with illness. Airing our feelings can fortify, not devastate, a relationship. By gravitating toward opposing stances on so many daily issues, James and Grace were preventing themselves from turning toward and bolstering each other. Grace was too angry about what was happening to her and too caught up in directing that anger at James to thank him for assisting, driving, and even comforting her at times. He resented her for that and was feeling stressed and a little sorry for himself. James didn't need a medal for being a hero, but he could have used a pat on the back. In fact, a University at Buffalo study found that showing appreciation can help alleviate the burden of spousal caregiving.

The challenges to couples caring for aging parents are different. Time devoted to a parent is time taken away from the marital relationship. Sometimes couples tolerate this well, with both spouses pitching in. But sometimes, one spouse begrudges—openly or subtly—the time the other partner spends with a parent. This only places more pressure on the caregiving spouse, who is already under duress.

We know one colleague whose husband kept encouraging her to hire help to take her eighty-six-year-old mother to medical appointments and stay with her during intermittent hospitalizations. Our colleague explained calmly that she could best take care of her mother and that as long as she had the time, she would. She also shared how hard it was for her to care for her mother and watch her decline and asked for his support. In time, he came to understand that this was an important priority for the entire family. He began supporting her visits and even joining her occasionally.

Unless the couple communicates about the caregiving burdens, shares the responsibilities, and finds other sources of support, caregiving can put a strain on their relationship. If the eldercare continues for years, it can impact their finances, health outcomes, social life, and intimate relationship and undermine the caregiver's health.

Grieving the Loss of Loved Ones and the Loss of Intimacy

Dealing with a chronic or serious illness is about coping with loss. The person with the illness loses abilities, confidence, and a sense of identity. If you're caregiving for a spouse, you may feel like you've lost the partner you fell in love with and shared a life with for decades.

Nowhere is this more clearly seen than in the couple's intimacy. Spousal caregivers can become so wrapped up in the tasks of caregiving that they neglect to share their thoughts and feelings, unwittingly sacrificing emotional closeness. Physical intimacy—not just sexual relations but cuddling and other forms of physical affection—may become limited by the illness, side effects of medications and treatments, and the caregiver's sheer exhaustion. The shifts in roles can also undermine desire, especially if one spouse is bathing or toileting the other. It is extremely difficult for a well spouse to function as a nurse at one moment and a lover the next.

Psychologist Linda Mona recommends that spousal caregivers try to separate those roles as much as possible—literally. She suggests wearing one hat or outfit while caregiving and another while just being a spouse—say, watching a movie together or holding hands. By compartmentalizing in this fashion, spousal caregivers may be able to create the right circumstances to protect and maintain intimacy in their relationship. But transitioning between both roles to protect desire is still difficult. You can't always predict when caregiving needs and emergencies will arise, making it nearly impossible to ensure that a given time period will be strictly devoted to nurturing the relationship.

James and Grace were struggling with this. Affection between them had faded away. They had always fallen back on their intimacy in the past to feel closer. Now that felt uncomfortable.

But there was an even bigger issue. James feared losing both his wife and his father. The grief weighed on him. Grace would likely die before him. In those moments of reflection, James felt his deep love for Grace. He also faced the fear of being alone one day. With this concern in mind, some caregivers begin distancing themselves emotionally and physically from the person they're caring for—even while that person is still present. Unfortunately, they then often experience markedly guilty feelings later ("Why wasn't I there for her when she needed me?").

Spouses can't control the future; they can only make the most of their time together now. That means more moments of closeness, not fewer. As we tell couples in this circumstance, make the memories today that you want to cherish tomorrow. That kind of cherishing, writes psychologist Polly Young-Eisendrath in her book *The Present*

Heart, may be the most important and lasting type of intimacy we can manage during the caregiving years.

Restoring Joy

Despite a marriage filled with bickering, James and Grace had always found ways to create small moments of joy by watching old movies together, taking a walk around the block after dinner, or simply hanging around with their kids and grandkids. But since Grace's health had become so much worse and their life together had become harder, they'd almost forgotten that they could make each other a little happier. Without any joy, the moments of anger and bitterness seemed to exacerbate their frustrations and pain.

Although caregiving is full of problems, disappointments, and frustrations, look for places and moments to find joy. Amy Goyer, an AARP caregiving expert who has been a family caregiver most of her life, suggests that caregivers and care receivers purposely strive to find joyful moments. It is like building a reserve of love and goodwill to draw on to keep going forward through adversity. Engaging in activities that bring joy needn't take a lot of time or money.

You can watch movies together or listen to your favorite music. You can play board or card games or do puzzles together. You can laugh at a humorous comedian on television, or give each other massages. You can go on local adventures and travel. You'll want to make sure that a museum is wheelchair accessible or has plenty of benches if you're working around mobility limitations, for example. Parks often have paved trails. Many couples we know just enjoy going for a drive together. These activities can bring sweetness and lightness to your relationship.

Goyer recommends that caregivers and care receivers keep a "joy journal" to note positive, happy, and memorable moments. It is one more way to cherish each other more. Invariably, this will prove to be comforting in the future by referring back to the book whenever second-guessing and guilt start to arise. If it's with a parent, the grandchildren can continue to enjoy it.

Tying It All Together

Barry looked at James and Grace. "I know that you love each other and that this time has been challenging to both of you," he said. "Let's start with you, Grace. What do you think you can do to make it easier for James?"

Grace thought for a moment and then slowly answered, "I could probably do what he asks more often without giving him such a hard time. He asks me to take my pills over and over until I do. He pressures me to eat when I don't feel like it. He tells me not to go upstairs unless he is there to help me."

"So," said Barry, "if you did what he asks more, he'd have an easier time and might be less controlling."

"Yeah. Probably," she said.

Barry asked her, "What do you need from James?"

"I need him to let me do some things. Ask my opinion. I want to be able to look at the finances. I want to go shopping with him or at least make the list."

Barry turned to James. "It feels like Grace needs to feel useful and included."

"A lot of times it's easier if I just do things myself," James explained, "but I see what you're saying."

They decided to do the bills together. Grace would write the shopping list. She'd also call James's father from time to time to chat with him when they knew he'd be alone.

Then James said, "Maybe if I do this for her, then she could do what I want, like watch a movie with me and not complain the whole time."

Maybe if Grace could be more helpful, she'd feel less helpless and resistant, Barry explained. And James could have an easier time getting everything done, even if it took a bit longer. More time doing things together might help them feel closer. And more times choosing activities that they enjoyed together would balance out the tougher times. Maybe they'd both feel less resentful and more like a team. James also agreed to talk about his sadness about his dad, and Grace agreed to listen. They could get through almost everything, Barry told them, by simply being there and feeling compassion for each other.

How to Address Your Caregiving Concerns

If you and your partner are caregiving or expect to be, consider taking the following Check-Up.

You and your partner should fill out the Check-Up separately and then compare your results. There are no right or wrong answers, only places where you and your partner have diverging or similar feelings, experiences, or needs. All are important to know about. The divergent places are opportunities to share and learn so that you can plan mindfully how to handle caregiving issues now and in the future.

CAREGIVING CHECK-UP

1. My partner and I discuss caregiving needs, whether for each other or for relatives or friends.

Strongly Disagree   Disagree   Neutral   Agree   Strongly Agree

2. My partner and I share our responsibilities caring for relatives or friends.

Strongly Disagree   Disagree   Neutral   Agree   Strongly Agree

3. My partner and I feel committed to each other no matter what the future holds.

Strongly Disagree   Disagree   Neutral   Agree   Strongly Agree

4. My partner and I make sure we have intimacy, even when there are limitations.

Strongly Disagree   Disagree   Neutral   Agree   Strongly Agree

5. My partner and I talk about our feelings of loss.

Strongly Disagree   Disagree   Neutral   Agree   Strongly Agree

6. My partner and I discuss how caregiving does or could affect our finances.

Strongly Disagree   Disagree   Neutral   Agree   Strongly Agree

7. My partner and I are able to ask for help with caregiving when we need it.

Strongly Disagree   Disagree   Neutral   Agree   Strongly Agree

8. My partner and I accept help when it is offered.

Strongly Disagree   Disagree   Neutral   Agree   Strongly Agree

9. My partner and I have supportive friends, neighbors, and family we can ask for help.

Strongly Disagree   Disagree   Neutral   Agree   Strongly Agree

10. My partner and I ask for help with caregiving duties.

    Strongly Disagree   Disagree   Neutral   Agree   Strongly Agree

11. My partner and I discuss end-of-life planning with each other.

    Strongly Disagree   Disagree   Neutral   Agree   Strongly Agree

12. My partner and I discuss end-of-life planning with our families.

    Strongly Disagree   Disagree   Neutral   Agree   Strongly Agree

13. My partner and I can adjust our plans to accommodate caregiving needs.

    Strongly Disagree   Disagree   Neutral   Agree   Strongly Agree

14. My partner and I rethink the future together to make it as meaningful as possible.

    Strongly Disagree   Disagree   Neutral   Agree   Strongly Agree

15. My partner and I support each other to the best of our ability.

    Strongly Disagree   Disagree   Neutral   Agree   Strongly Agree

16. My partner and I consult with medical experts for health-related concerns.

    Strongly Disagree   Disagree   Neutral   Agree   Strongly Agree

17. My partner and I feel like we are part of a supportive community.

    Strongly Disagree   Disagree   Neutral   Agree   Strongly Agree

18. My partner and I talk about future options if caregiving gets too challenging.

    Strongly Disagree   Disagree   Neutral   Agree   Strongly Agree

19. My partner and I create moments of joy when we can.

    Strongly Disagree   Disagree   Neutral   Agree   Strongly Agree

20. My partner and I tell each other that we love each other, even when things get difficult.

    Strongly Disagree   Disagree   Neutral   Agree   Strongly Agree

Reviewing the Caregiving Check-Up

If you have five or more widely diverging answers (on opposite sides of the "neutral" choice): You probably need to address your caregiving issues and the differences in your perspectives.

If you diverge on numbers 1, 2, 7, 8, and 15: You probably aren't talking enough about your personal needs and wishes regarding caregiving and how you can best support each other.

If you don't agree on numbers 3, 4, 6, 11, 17, and 18: It may be time to sit down and have those difficult conversations, take a hard look at your current or future situation, reach compromises, and make decisions together so that both of you get your needs met now and down the road.

If you're far apart on numbers 19 or 20: You may want to take stock together of your dedication to the success of your relationship.

Next Steps

If you want to try to improve your emotional connection as you care for a loved one or each other and increase your ability to cooperate and negotiate to meet the needs of both of you, you'll want to try to be patient as you listen to each other and share your thoughts and feelings. This is an opportunity to get to know one another deeply regarding current and future caregiving concerns. If you both agree to take your time with it, you will get the most from it. Here's what we suggest:

Make an appointment with each other to sit down together for an hour. You won't be making big decisions; you'll be sharing your Check-Up results and talking about where you agree and disagree.

Take turns telling each other how you feel about your caregiving concerns. Read over the "Tips for Talking and Listening" found at the beginning of this book. The process may feel slow and labored, but you'll see that taking the time to carefully approach this difficult conversation will pay off. Take turns telling each other how you feel about being a caregiver, being a care receiver, or the grief about the losses you may be feeling.

Let yourselves be vulnerable. Caregiving is often fraught with ambivalence. It is a way to demonstrate love and to feel that life has meaning. But it is difficult work, often imbued with painful feelings of fear and loss. Care receivers can feel less-than, angry about their feelings of helplessness, resentful about needing care, and even painfully grateful. Do your best to listen patiently, quietly, and nonjudgmentally. Give your partner time to talk.

Respond to your partner with a validating comment, even if you feel surprised or upset. Just listen closely and summarize what your partner said, so you both feel heard. Be respectful and supportive. You aren't solving problems now; you are sharing feelings and learning about each other.

A Week Later

Sharing your feelings, frustrations, hopes, and fears about your caregiving experiences will help you feel that you are working together as a team. You are carefully creating a caregiving experience that is as positive and meaningful as possible.

About a week after you discuss your Check-Up results, meet again to share any additional reactions to your findings and begin formulating a plan to improve your caregiving experience.

Here are some questions to spur your conversation:

- How can you improve the balance in your relationship?
- If you are sharing in the care for a family member, how can you support each other?
- What can you do together to avoid feeling overburdened?
- Can you ask relatives or friends to chip in?
- Does the care receiver feel satisfied with his or her care?
- Does the caregiver feel satisfied with his or her caregiving?
- How do you deal with intimacy issues?
- Are you feeling resentment now that your roles have shifted?
- How can you better manage your financial concerns?
- Do you have a support network that will help you take some time to refuel?
- Do you make time together and apart to engage in something fun that brings joy?
- How can you help each other achieve your goals and build more meaning into your lives?
- What do each of you want and need?

Remember that your goal is to feel more connected and accepting of how each of you feel about this challenging issue. Reflect on how your conversation went and commit to continuing to share your feelings. Find compromises to improve the experiences of both of you with regard to caregiving.

End the hour by trying to set a positive goal, whether it's a planned break from the pressures of caregiving to do something fun together or a new approach to an old challenge so that caregiving can feel more like a joint effort.

An Ongoing Plan to Integrate Change

We've found that lasting change doesn't really take hold unless you also spend time reviewing and fine-tuning the plan you've created. Schedule a regular meeting not just to be together but to reflect on how your relationship is going. Checking in can feel awkward at first, but you'll soon find that it can be comforting and nourishing to your relationship, an opportunity to feel connected.

Talk about how you both feel about what you have learned about each other. Integrating caregiving into your life together is a challenge. It can bring you closer, but it can add stress to a relationship. Continue communicating about what works and what doesn't for each of you. You don't have to agree, but you should be accepting and respectful as you continue to work on your changing relationship. Your goal is to feel more connected as you go through this process. Even if you continue to work on areas in which you disagree, try to share feelings, remember shared experiences, grieve together, and aim for compromise and good boundaries. Find joy wherever you can together as you support each other through the challenges of caregiving.

Steps to Success

We recommend that you do your best to keep the lines of communication open. Check in with each other frequently to share feelings about how each of you are faring.

Keep the following steps in mind as you go:

- Strengthen your emotional bond through sharing feelings and setting aside times to talk about difficult feelings, past and present.
- Listen without judgment.

- Grieve together when necessary.
- Plan activities together and pursue new experiences.
- Negotiate time together and apart.
- Have conversations about the future.
- Look for opportunities to experience joy together.

Listen to each other closely and show compassion for each other as you manage this extremely challenging life shift. Talk to each other frequently about how you are both doing so that you can flexibly adjust, to the best of your ability, to changing needs. If you are the care receiver, try to continue to offer whatever care to the caregiver that you can. You may not be able to cook or clean, but you can listen and offer emotional support. If you are the caregiver, build a support network so that you can let others help out to provide emotional support and take a break. Bring in family, neighbors, members of your house of worship, and friends. Give others an opportunity to contribute. It is always helpful to have other people to talk to and learn from. Caregiving is a difficult task, but it can also be the most meaningful thing you'll ever do.

Challenge 10

Loss of Loved Ones

To Barry's surprise, James showed up for his marital therapy appointment alone and looking disheveled and exhausted. Barry braced himself for bad news about Grace. But James brought up a different loss: His father, ninety-two, had died of a heart attack.

Since then, James said, he had had trouble sleeping, could barely hold a conversation, and snapped at Grace more than usual. He didn't want to take out his pain on her but couldn't seem to stop himself. And while she knew he was hurting, she was sniping back, angry at him for scapegoating her. They knew they needed Barry's help.

Facing loss is a universal task. If you've loved, then it's likely that you've felt the pain of loss. There are so many losses we are likely to face as we go through life. Our children move away for school or jobs. We move, experiencing the loss of home and community. When we retire, we lose our work identity. We may face changes in our health— another loss. Then there's the loss of loved ones who die. We are likely to have to experience the deaths of our parents. Some have to face the tragic death of their children as well as other relatives and friends.

It can feel like the losses pile up quickly. Feelings of helplessness, sadness, and grief can upend the normal rhythms of relationships. In our practices, we help couples deal with how to absorb these losses together and maintain a supportive attitude toward each other when their grief—and often the responsibilities that come with a loved one's demise—overwhelms them.

Facing the loss together is an opportunity for you to feel more connected. If you can support each other through your grief, share your pain, and empathize with each other about your losses, then you can become stronger and more resilient and grow closer. But many partners avoid talking about or sharing their grief and grow apart. In our work with grieving couples, we focus on the following three steps to strengthen relationships: feeling your feelings, building resilience, and making meaning out of loss. But just a note before we go on: If you are struggling with grief, consider seeking help through bereavement counselors and group or individual psychotherapy.

Feeling Your Feelings

The loss of a loved one can overwhelm a survivor with distressing thoughts. The activities that brought him joy may now seem meaningless. Grief can make him question the point and direction of his own life. It is hard for a partner to witness a spouse suffering in this way. It is harder still when that spouse, preoccupied with these thoughts, has withdrawn from the relationship to such an extent that he seems unreachable.

That's what happened with Jeff and Stacy, Julia's clients. Stacy's mother had passed away several months before. To cope with the pain, she compulsively played games on her phone every day. When Jeff tried to talk to her, she'd barely make eye contact or respond. As the therapy progressed, Stacy admitted that she feared her grief would never stop once she opened the floodgates. Slowly, she began to express her feelings, and eventually she no longer needed to lose herself in her phone.

Shutting down and avoiding emotions is a short-term fix with long-term negative consequences. To heal grief and prevent it from damaging a relationship, spouses have to grapple with the messy and sometimes-conflicting feelings that come up—not just sadness, anger, and guilt but even more uncomfortable emotions, such as relief. Though many people judge themselves about the feelings that arise, trying to control them will only prolong or derail the grieving process.

The effects on the relationship are often compounded by the survivor's guilt because he's still alive while a loved one has died. He may feel heartbroken about having to handle responsibilities such as auctioning off or discarding parents' belongings, even keepsakes collected over a lifetime. Or he may have unwanted, recurring, and upsetting visual images of the parent just before or after death, if it was an especially traumatic one—what psychologists call post-traumatic stress symptoms. All these feelings can be disorienting and leave a bereft survivor feeling detached, confused, and even angry.

The anger is especially challenging for couples to manage. The grieving spouse may feel angry at the world or at the injustice of the loss, or he may struggle with old, complicated feelings about the lost loved one. He may unwittingly take out his frustration about the loss on his partner, feeling that no one can fill the gap the lost loved one left. These feelings of grief can be so extreme and often irrational that, rather than supporting each other through mourning, the spouses may find themselves arguing and blaming each other for unrelated, usually minor, offenses. Because anger is often easier to tolerate than sadness, couples can get locked in an angry pattern that doesn't help them work through their feelings of grief when they should be sharing feelings empathically.

Knowing James and Grace's tendency toward blaming and arguing, Barry was concerned that this dynamic had gripped them after the death of James's father. Barry knew that the best way he could help them now was to encourage James to experience and express the sadness that was likely being subconsciously diverted into anger. He looked at him sitting on his couch and said sympathetically, "I'm so sorry, James. It looks like you're having a hard time grieving this sudden loss. Would you like to talk about your dad?"

James shrugged and responded quietly, "I don't know where to start."

"I'm sure finding him was upsetting," Barry said. "Could you tell me about what happened?"

At first, he protested that there was no point in going through it again. Like many mourners, he had avoided thinking about the death. In fact, he had avoided thinking about much of anything at all. But now he told Barry about the circumstances leading up to his dad's death: the weeks before—a car accident due to heart failure, the hospitalization, the discharge with the doctor's order to not drive and to get help with meals and bathing at home, the brothers taking turns helping out with their father—up to finding him in his bed, unresponsive. He shared with Barry the terror he had felt and, since then, the exhaustion, inattentiveness, and forgetfulness.

Barry listened carefully, letting James describe what it was like for him to find his father. As James shared the story, he relived some of his horror, with Barry as witness this time. Barry's supportive words comforted him, and he was able to calm down again.

He went on to report that Grace found him frustrating. She wanted to support him, but he seemed to have pulled far into himself. He couldn't tell her what he needed. She couldn't read his mind.

He then admitted to Barry that he felt very angry with Grace. On the morning of his father's fatal heart attack, she'd delayed him because she hadn't wanted to get out of bed to get ready for dialysis. If Grace had hurried up like she was supposed to and if James had gotten to his father's house an hour earlier, then maybe he could have been able to save his dad somehow. He knew that his wife hadn't indirectly caused his father's death, but he couldn't shake his anger at her.

As they spoke, James was able to recognize that he felt guilty that he had let his father and his brothers down. They had been relying on him, and he had failed. Like other times in his life, he felt like a disappointment. As James started crying, Barry knew he was beginning to acknowledge his painful feelings of self-blame—feelings that were intensifying and that, unexpressed, would prolong his grief. It was a good start, but James had a long way to go.

As Barry and James came to the end of their session together, it was clear to both of them that James had been afraid to let himself feel the guilt, frustration, and overwhelming sadness inside him. Like many people, he seemed to be trying to set aside his grief by avoiding, minimizing, or denying it.

Building Resilience

When partners don't share their feelings, however painful, they can begin to feel less close and trusting. There is no road map for grief and no expiration date for how long those feelings last. The idea that grief occurs in predictable stages has long been rejected and replaced by more expansive theories that account for how cultural norms, spiritual views, and individual outlooks shape unique grief experiences. Some people see a relatively quick diminution of feelings over several months to a year. Others never completely recover. Whatever you experience is normal.

Spouses tend to fall back on old ways of coping whenever they encounter stress, especially when they are facing a loss. To maintain or rebuild closeness, partners will need to face these old behavior patterns and make the effort to build in better skills for managing their feelings and expressing them constructively.

Research on resilience during times of loss and grief has found that people who grieve successfully tend to have a sense of acceptance about death and believe that the world is a just place. Those who have a hard time grieving tend to have dependency issues even before experiencing loss. For them, loss can feel like abandonment. Every loss impacts each person differently. There is no one way to grieve. In our work, we focus on individual reactions and how they can affect couples, as well as what couples can do about it together.

As Grace pointed out in the couple's appointment with Barry the following week, she was grateful that James no longer seemed so angry at her, but she was concerned that he spent all his time at home channel surfing. "I think he's depressed," she said. "I just wish he would talk to me. I loved his father, too. I'm also grieving. It feels like James has disappeared. I feel all alone."

Barry suggested that Grace might be able to help James. "Why don't you sit next to James and let him know it's okay for him to be sad," he said, reassuringly. "You'll be there to comfort him."

Grace looked at her husband, put her arm around him, and said, "He knew you loved him. You were a really good son and did whatever you could for him. It was just his time. You didn't disappoint him or your brothers. It's okay."

We've found in our work with grief that people who tend to be optimistic, who generally believe that something good is likely to come from even the worst circumstances, have an easier time grieving. Those who aren't naturally optimistic can build resilience by focusing on what they are grateful for, positive outcomes that are actually possible, and their hopes rather than fears.

To better cope with loss, we suggest that couples reflect on how they are feeling, journal about their experiences, and allow others to comfort them. People who are resilient in grief also purposefully bring up positive memories of the person who passed away. Those memories provide a source of comfort.

Barry asked James to share an old memory of his father. James told the story of when he'd decided to drop out of college because he didn't see the value in doing all that work, and his father, who didn't even have a high school degree, helped him get over his fear of failing and stay in school. For that, James said, he felt forever grateful. Grace said to him, "Your dad was an amazing man."

James sat quietly, looking down. Tears came to his eyes. Slowly, he started to shake a little. When Grace realized he was crying, she hugged him closer and cried with him. Together, they would get through the pain of his dad's death.

When we provide counseling for partners struggling with unbearable loss and unresolved grief, we encourage them to turn toward, not away from, each other. We suggest they make the time to talk about that loss, their feelings, and their memories and to communicate together about them as much as they can. We believe this is necessary to truly understand each other's experiences and to support each other. Those experiences can include disappointment, regret, and self-blame but also good memories of the deceased in better days. What's most important is for spouses to listen and accept each other at this emotionally fraught time.

This is how long-term relationships develop increased closeness and resilience. If spouses can demonstrate that they're there for each other through this loss, then each will believe more deeply that the other will be there to provide understanding and acceptance whenever other losses and painful circumstances occur during their life together. The opposite is also true, of course. If a partner isn't emotionally there with steadfast love and support now, then who would reasonably count on her later?

Grace had taken steps to prove herself in Barry's office. But she had also surprised James. He didn't doubt that she missed his father but hadn't thought she was as upset about his loss as she'd said. What James didn't suspect was that his father's death had brought up overwhelming feelings of grief for Grace because of the losses of her parents and brother in the last decade. She had emotionally withdrawn from him as well because she hadn't wanted to bother James with her painful feelings while he was struggling with his own. When she was finally able to explain this to him, he expressed regret that she hadn't shared her feelings with him so that he could support her, too. Often, when we experience a loss, we reignite feelings of grief related to earlier losses. For many, these feelings can be overwhelming unless we share them.

We tell our clients that talking together about the loved ones they've lost is a way to honor them. Sharing fond memories helps them tolerate the losses and feel closer to the cherished people still around them. They increase their resilience and strengthen their relationships each time they face pain head-on and work through it with each other. Remembering occasions with the people they've lost will eventually feel good and can remind them that they still hold dear so much of who they were even when they're gone.

Making Meaning out of Loss

With each loss we suffer, we have the potential to commune around our grief and grow together. Family and cultural rituals, such as sitting shiva, holding a wake, or having a memorial mass or a celebration of life, can bolster that sense of togetherness. They can give us a feeling of belonging, provide a supportive community to stand shoulder to shoulder with us, and be a community-sanctioned means for expressing our intense feelings.

In our psychotherapy practices, we have seen that mourning can be a source of personal growth for the bereaved. Has the person strengthened connections with others, followed the advice of the person who died, carried on a tradition, or created something new that somehow relates to the loss? Has grief led the bereaved down a new path?

Research about bereavement in older adults found that people who have a strong social network and religious beliefs or a sense of spirituality tend to cope better after loss. Death brings increased sadness but also reminds us to value each other while we can. Mourners gain a new sense of perspective on mortality and feel a renewed sense of purpose for making the best use of their time. They are animated by new energy to engage in activities of greatest significance to them.

That often means devoting themselves to helping others, including spouses, who are of greatest significance to them, too. We've seen spouses grow in their ability to express empathy, understanding, patience, and compassion. More than anything else, they may feel increased gratitude for having supportive and loving people in their lives. The small frictions and annoyances of everyday life seem to matter less. In the best-case scenarios, they rededicate themselves to improving and deepening those relationships and making every moment together count.

Making meaning of our losses may also mean allowing others to give to us, too. Sometimes we feel too proud and independent, but it is often through receiving help that we most make others feel important. It is by helping each other that we create a sense of loving community.

Grace and James told Barry that more than a hundred friends, relatives, and members of their church community had attended the funeral, shared stories about his dad, and sent casseroles and fruit baskets, along with loving notes. And the pastor had asked to meet with James when he was ready.

Barry asked, "Ready for what?"

James smiled for the first time in the session. "When I'm ready, he wants me to lead a discussion for the youth group on fatherhood," he responded. "Because my father was such an exemplary man and I've tried to be a good father myself, he thought I'd be a good person for that. He told me the church community could use some of the wisdom I learned from my father."

Barry agreed that it would be a nice way for James to honor his father's life and make meaning of his death. James would also feel joy telling stories about his father. The pastor had made sure that Grace would be there, too, to listen, to support James, and to share her own stories about his father.

You can make meaning from loss in so many ways. You might volunteer with or make a memorial donation to an organization that the person supported. You might create a scrapbook with others to honor the person as you share stories. You could donate the deceased's artwork or other valuables. You could plant a tree, read poetry, light a candle, or just share photos and memories. Even wearing a piece of the person's jewelry or clothing can be comforting and remind you that your loved one's memory is always close by.

Tying It All Together

Nearly a year after James's father had passed away, he and Grace came in for a follow-up appointment with Barry. He suggested that they might want to commemorate the upcoming anniversary of James's father's death. Barry explained that many people find holidays, birthdays, and anniversaries to be difficult times after a loss, especially in the first year or two. He said that creating a communal ritual around loss can be affirming and rewarding.

"We could have a big picnic and do a slideshow," Grace suggested. "I bet the grandkids would love that."

James looked interested. Barry encouraged him to consider that as well as some other ways to reminisce about his father with his brothers and other relatives. Sharing pictures and stories would be a way for James to help his family continue to work through the loss as well as share some happy memories.

Barry could tell that as time had passed, they'd been coping with the death as they had with so many losses before. There would be bickering and crying, but the intensity of their painful feelings would continue to decrease. Going through it together had brought them closer to each other and prepared them to better handle losses in store for them in the future.

How to Address Your Concerns About Loss of Loved Ones

If you and your partner are going through feelings of loss and want to work on better addressing these difficult experiences together, consider taking the following Check-Up.

You and your partner should fill out the Check-Up separately and then compare your results. There are no right or wrong answers, only places where you and your partner may have diverging or similar feelings, experiences, or needs. All are important to know about. The divergent places are opportunities to share and learn so that you can plan mindfully how to manage loss together.

LOSS OF LOVED ONES CHECK-UP

1. My partner and I are able to grieve together for as long as it takes.

   Strongly Disagree   Disagree   Neutral   Agree   Strongly Agree

2. My partner and I give each other space to grieve alone when one of us needs it.

   Strongly Disagree   Disagree   Neutral   Agree   Strongly Agree

3. My partner and I talk about our feelings, even the most painful ones.

   Strongly Disagree   Disagree   Neutral   Agree   Strongly Agree

4. My partner and I recognize moodiness as an aspect of grief.

   Strongly Disagree   Disagree   Neutral   Agree   Strongly Agree

5. My partner and I try to find meaning in our losses.

   Strongly Disagree   Disagree   Neutral   Agree   Strongly Agree

6. My partner and I don't use alcohol, tranquilizers, or other substances to alleviate our grief.

   Strongly Disagree   Disagree   Neutral   Agree   Strongly Agree

7. My partner and I recognize that grief can affect emotional health and look for the signs.

   Strongly Disagree   Disagree   Neutral   Agree   Strongly Agree

8. My partner and I are open to getting support from a professional to work through grief.

   Strongly Disagree   Disagree   Neutral   Agree   Strongly Agree

9. My partner and I take care of ourselves, leaving time to grieve even when busy.

   Strongly Disagree   Disagree   Neutral   Agree   Strongly Agree

10. My partner and I don't lash out at each other as a way to release difficult feelings.

    Strongly Disagree   Disagree   Neutral   Agree   Strongly Agree

11. My partner and I talk about feelings of injustice, fear, trauma, and even relief regarding our loss.

    Strongly Disagree Disagree Neutral Agree Strongly Agree

12. My partner and I acknowledge that death can mean significant changes in our lives.

    Strongly Disagree Disagree Neutral Agree Strongly Agree

13. My partner and I avoid making life-altering decisions while we are grieving.

    Strongly Disagree Disagree Neutral Agree Strongly Agree

14. My partner and I are patient with each other and sensitive to each other's feelings.

    Strongly Disagree Disagree Neutral Agree Strongly Agree

15. My partner and I rely on our social networks so that we feel less alone in our grief.

    Strongly Disagree Disagree Neutral Agree Strongly Agree

16. My partner and I are reassuring to each other during this difficult time.

    Strongly Disagree Disagree Neutral Agree Strongly Agree

17. My partner and I watch each other for signs of loss of interest in others and activities.

    Strongly Disagree Disagree Neutral Agree Strongly Agree

18. My partner and I honor loved ones we have lost with rituals and remembrances.

    Strongly Disagree Disagree Neutral Agree Strongly Agree

19. My partner and I mindfully create meaning in our lives every day.

    Strongly Disagree Disagree Neutral Agree Strongly Agree

20. My partner and I feel grateful for the life we have together.

    Strongly Disagree Disagree Neutral Agree Strongly Agree

Reviewing the Loss of Loved Ones Check-Up

If you have five or more widely diverging answers (on opposite sides of the "neutral" choice): You probably need to spend some time addressing your issues regarding loss and grief.

If you differ significantly on numbers 1, 2, 3, 8, and 14: You need to work on supporting each other emotionally and being sensitive to your partner's needs. Take the time to listen and share feelings without judgment.

If you diverge on numbers 5, 11, 12, and 19: You likely need to spend more time understanding the losses you are experiencing and sharing the meaning they have for each of you. Try to help each other find meaning in the losses you are facing and build meaning into your lives.

If you don't agree on numbers 6, 7, 9, 13, 15, and 18: One or both of you may be avoiding the grieving process by focusing on activities that provide short-term comfort but can lead ultimately to depression, anxiety, feelings of isolation, and strains within your relationship. Life is full of losses. These experiences can bring couples closer together or lead to painful distancing within relationships. Make sure you are working to connect with each other as you grieve.

Next Steps

If you want to support each other more and try to improve your emotional connection as you experience and integrate grief and loss, here's what we suggest:

Make an appointment to sit down together for an hour. You won't be making big decisions; you'll be sharing your Check-Up results and talking about where you agree and disagree. Take turns sharing your grief over the losses you may feel and how you feel you and your partner have handled them. Talk about what you need, what would be helpful to you, and how you can help each other through the pain of loss.

Let yourselves be vulnerable. Do your best to listen patiently, quietly, and nonjudgmentally. Give your partner time to talk. Remember that this isn't easy for either of you. End the hour by identifying areas of agreement from the Check-Up. Try to feel confident that you will work out your differences and reach compromises as you continue to talk together.

Respond to your partner with a validating comment, even if you feel surprised or upset. Just listen closely and summarize what your partner said, so you both feel heard. Be respectful and supportive. You aren't solving problems now; you are sharing feelings and learning about each other.

Remember that your goal is to feel more connected. End the hour by identifying areas of agreement from the Check-Up and setting a positive goal. Try to create a ritual in which both of you can honor your loss together. This will be an opportunity to feel closer.

A Week Later

About a week after you discuss your Check-Up results, meet again to share any additional reactions to your findings and begin formulating a plan to improve your relationship. You are sharing your feelings, learning about each other, and trying to make meaning regarding loss together so that you can feel closer.

Here are some questions to spur your conversation:

- Do you listen to each other and show that you understand your partner's feelings by reflecting back what you've heard?

- Are you frustrated by your partner's avoidance of grief?

- Can you agree to make time to talk about your memories and to honor those you've lost?

- How do each of you find support? Is it from others, or do you avoid others when you are suffering? How can you help each other?

- Can you try to be mindfully present for each other even when feelings are excruciating?

- Will you work together to create ways to find meaning regarding your losses?

- Can you plan to spend time together engaged in something that you both value as a way of communing around loss?

- Will you develop a ritual that allows you both to focus your feelings about the lost loved one?

An Ongoing Plan to Integrate Change

Plan to meet again as many times as necessary to talk about how you are both feeling about the losses you have been experiencing and how supported you feel within your relationship. Remember, grief has no timetable. Share what you have learned about how each of you manages loss and what each of you needs from your partner as well as from others. You don't have to agree about every detail, but you should be accepting and respectful as you continue to work on your deepening relationship. Your goal is to feel more connected regarding the difficult feelings of loss. Going through loss together can bring you closer if you continue to share feelings and support each other. Even if you disagree on how to manage your pain or don't fully understand the intensity of your partner's feelings, try to keep sharing, remember shared experiences, grieve together, and aim for connection.

Steps to Success

As you continue to work together to process loss, deepen your connection, and create meaning, keep the following in mind:

- Accept your and your partner's feelings no matter how complicated they may be, how much they fluctuate, or how long they last.
- Reflect on whether you or your partner are withdrawing and isolating rather than connecting.
- Share your feelings of vulnerability and your fears about mortality.
- Build personal strength and resilience through sharing and caring for others.
- Create rituals to honor the lost and connect to those around you.
- Increase your sense of your own life significance through the pursuit of meaningful endeavors.

Ultimately, loss can bring a new perspective to the life cycle. Intimately sharing both the gains and losses that occur throughout our lives can bring us closer to our partners. While we may suffer and struggle, inevitably these experiences can bring a stronger connection and help us create meaning from the difficult losses that we face over our life span.

When Nothing Works

Cooperative Separation and Divorce

Sometimes relationships need to end. That's the sad truth. If you've walked through the challenges that apply to you and have ended up here, your relationship may need to draw to a close. You may be considering a separation and eventual divorce.

First, though, ask yourselves:

- Have we frankly talked about our differences and difficulties?
- Have we let down our defenses and truly listened to each other?
- Have we explored every avenue we could think of to make things work, including going through this book and working with a professional?

If you answer yes to these questions and are unable to make the progress you need to make your marriage strong and satisfying, then keep reading.

We approach the topic of separation and divorce with caution and care because it can be so challenging in so many ways. No matter how you handle the process, there is always loss that comes with the end of an important relationship.

While many people who leave unhappy marriages feel relief afterward, the process will likely be agonizing. On the stress scale of the most difficult life changes, divorce is number two and marital separation is number three. Only death of a spouse or child is more stressful. The death of another close family member, at number five, is less stressful than divorce.

Even with the small solace that you gave it your all and now agree that your marriage just can't work, separation causes emotional upheaval, disruption of your everyday life, and often extreme feelings of grief. Shame and disappointment, uncertainty about finances and the future, fears about loneliness: These feelings and more can also accompany the transition. If the split is contentious, the experience is even worse. Unfortunately, the divorce rate for couples over fifty is on the rise, doubling from 1990 to 2015, according to a Pew Research Foundation study, while the divorce rate for those over sixty-five has tripled since 1990. We face a tidal wave of "gray divorce," as it's been dubbed, says researcher Jocelyn Elise Crowley.

The rise in divorce among middle-aged and older adults affects not only the health and well-being of those who experience it directly. It can also have deep ramifications for the well-being of children, grandchildren, and extended family, notes Susan Brown of the National Center for Family & Marriage Research.

Our focus in psychotherapy starts with how separation and divorce impact the people directly involved. The acknowledgment of what may feel like time wasted, the recognition of having tolerated poor treatment and lived through betrayal or slow drift, the sense that you no longer really know the person you've been with for years, the feeling that you've not been true to yourself—all contribute to intense feelings of loss. Your sense of identity shifts when a relationship comes to an end. The sense of "we," the joint mission, and the dreams of a future together all disintegrate. You can feel unsure of who you are. You can feel like a failure.

Many couples are eager to leave the past behind and to separately start over as soon as possible. But healing from hurt requires an understanding of the past and an unhurried consideration of goals for the future. Ultimately, working their way out of a relationship can variously lead to ongoing pain and suffering or peace of mind for themselves and those around them, depending on how the separating partners handle their interactions.

In our practices, we try to help couples move forward in the most positive, healthy way possible. If they choose to walk away, they can do so in a manner that honors themselves, their relationship, their histories, and their families. They just have to take it step-by-step, moving from discord to acceptance, coming together to part, reflecting on the positives, and separating without severing.

Nevertheless, it's rarely an easy decision to walk away from the relationship. For most couples over fifty, it usually takes two years or more for one or both spouses to decide to separate. And again, please rely on professional help when appropriate.

From Discord to Acceptance

Barry ushered Nina and Ryan into his office for an initial meeting. On the phone, Nina had said they wanted couples therapy, but not to fix their relationship. They'd already tried that several years earlier with a different therapist and it hadn't helped. Instead, what they now wanted was a low-stress divorce. They had an adult daughter and two grandchildren, extended family, and plenty of friends in common. They wanted to make it as pain-free as possible for everyone.

When they sat down on Barry's couch, though, it immediately became clear that Ryan wasn't on board.

"She blindsided me," he said. "I thought things were pretty okay. We went to therapy, so I assumed things were better. Now these past weeks, she's saying she hasn't been happy for years."

As we've seen more and more in our psychotherapy practices and heard from colleagues, it is often women in heterosexual relationships who initiate divorce, usually as a result of long-term unhappiness with the marriages they've been in—typically marriages where the husband and wife have traditional male-female roles. The women are no longer comfortable with the power imbalances in their relationships and cannot convince their partners to shift them.

Another reason we often hear for a relationship's dissolution: slow drift, a catch-all term that reflects how couples have lost intimacy over the years, often without realizing it. The causes include avoiding confrontation, not sharing emotions, harboring long-standing resentments, not spending meaningful time together, having incompatibile interests, experiencing changes in life direction, sharing little to no sexual intimacy, and struggling with poor communication. Often, when a major life change occurs, such as when they retire or their children leave home, these couples find themselves feeling the lack of closeness more keenly. A spouse's annoying habits, behaviors, or assumptions become intolerable without the distractions of children or work and without the cushion of intimacy.

Although Ryan was taken by surprise by Nina's unilateral decision to divorce, he and Nina had experienced the same slow drift many long-term couples do. She had tried to help him understand this during their previous couples therapy sessions. In her mind, they no longer shared either emotional closeness or common interests. She liked Ryan—she even loved him—and didn't blame him. But at age sixty-six, she explained, she hoped to live at least another twenty years and wanted more from relationships than what they had.

He couldn't understand her dissatisfaction. Like many men, he rarely discussed his feelings. He didn't experience the same lack in their relationship. And, he said vehemently, he absolutely couldn't understand how she could consider splitting up and putting them both in economic jeopardy when they'd worked so hard to achieve financial stability.

"She's ruining my life," he said.

With that, Ryan stood up, strode across the room, and left the office.

Barry turned to Nina. "I think you need to give him some time to adjust to what's happening," he said.

Nina replied, "I've been trying to do that for weeks."

But a few weeks later, a calmer Ryan returned. He felt hurt; he felt rejected. But he was ready to adjust his expectations.

Coming Together to Part

Ryan's initial concern was financial. In fact, in the intervening weeks, he'd talked with an attorney about a financial agreement to divvy up their assets. He felt sick about it, he said. He'd worked hard all his life for his money and now Nina would be getting some of his retirement and half the house. Neither of them would now have enough money to afford comfortable retirements.

One of the greatest impacts of gray divorce is financial. When couples over fifty divorce, their wealth drops by around 50 percent, according to the National Center for Family & Marriage Research. For women, the standard of living dives 45 percent; for men, 21 percent. These declines are much larger than those for younger couples.

Because women often earn less than men, they tend to struggle more financially after the divorce. Research shows that they never recover from this financial hit; they just don't have the remaining time to bounce back to their former standard of living.

Nina said she understood the financial impact of their separation, but she explained to Ryan that she valued her well-being over her financial status. Ryan looked at her, baffled and anxious.

When couples begin the separation and divorce process, financial concerns, fears about the future, feelings of anger at perceived or real betrayal, and other anxieties about change can make emotions run high. When spouses can sit down together and talk through their feelings, needs, and hopes for the future, they may be able to work through their pain to reach a level of peace that will allow them to proceed more effectively. In our practices, we help separating couples focus on their goals for the future, given the changes they are facing.

Watching Ryan and Nina at a standstill over finances, Barry asked if they were willing to try something different. They agreed.

He encouraged them to listen closely to each other as they spoke about how they were feeling, but insisted they not complain about the past. As they took turns expressing their fears and anxieties, they began to recognize that they were both struggling, although in different ways. They aired their feelings, and Barry encouraged them to try to set aside old betrayals, hurts, and disappointments, which can be barriers to moving forward.

At their next session, Barry guided them to think more broadly, considering minimizing the impact on their family and social circle.

Their daughter, Anna, was married and had children of her own, and it was important to both of them to keep Anna and her family in their life and to convey a united, calm front. They didn't need to bring their family into the divorce drama and upset them.

"Parent–adult child relationship dynamics often change following parental marital dissolution," says Susan Brown of the National Center for Family & Marriage Research. "Divorced older adults no longer have a spouse on whom to rely and are likely to place greater demands on their children for social support. And children may be called on to serve as caregivers in lieu of a spouse. The strain of such intense obligations may weaken intergenerational ties."

Because divorce will impact their lives and the well-being of everyone around them, partners need to proceed gingerly. Even when a couple has had years of full-blown animosity between them, we recommend that they call a truce, work to accept their mistakes and losses, try to forgive each other or at least set the past aside, and focus on the challenges ahead. If couples can accomplish that, as difficult as it may sound, it will lead to a much better outcome for all involved for years to come.

By the time they left Barry's office, Nina and Ryan had agreed that although they were both still feeling vulnerable and emotional, they had to accept the fact that their lives would be changing in many ways. They would slowly come to terms with the dissolution of their marriage. They would learn to live with fewer financial resources. And they would try to minimize the negative impact on their family and friends. They committed to each other to work toward a cooperative divorce.

Reflecting on the Positives

In our practices, we help couples see that successfully working through separation and divorce can have a large positive ripple effect. Family members won't feel caught in the middle. Holidays and vacations won't be fraught. Graduations, weddings, and other important family occasions won't be awkward because the two divorced people are trying to avoid each other. Their social circles will feel less inclined to choose one partner over the other. That will make it easier to maintain friendships. Eventually, even the chance interactions of ex-spouses can be opportunities to catch up rather than act out long-held antagonism.

One key is to develop a positive perspective on your relationship. Focus on joyful times that you had together in the past. The experience of being a couple will come to an end. But other growth will follow.

When Nina and Ryan returned to Barry's office, Ryan reported that he'd come home from work and was surprised to see Nina waiting for him in the living room. She asked him if he would join her for a glass of wine. After a stunned moment, he agreed.

When he sat down, Nina told him she was feeling sad remembering good times with him. She brought up memories of Anna's childhood, family vacations, sporting events, and graduations they'd attended. As they spoke, both felt sad. Nina acknowledged that she was scared about the future. After all these years together, the adjustment to separation and self-reliance would be difficult. But she hoped they could hold on to the good parts of their life together. And she hoped they might both find more happiness ahead.

As they described the evening to Barry, their faces were grave. Their sense of sadness permeated the room. It made Barry feel optimistic about them. If they could grieve their marriage, they each stood a good chance of being able to go forward, unencumbered by regrets, and find peace.

Separating Without Severing

Something transformative can occur when spouses savor parts of their past together even as they move toward a clean separation. We urge partners to separate without severing—their day-to-day relationship may have ended, but their emotional relationship continues to evolve and affect them.

Divorce means the end of a particular kind of relationship. Their agreement is null and void. The challenge is to alter the connection while still honoring it. This allows them both to move on to the next stage of life, where they can respect each other and acknowledge that they have spent years of their lives together for better and for worse. Children, extended family, and friends will all appreciate their ability to be at the same events without trouble or concern. As time passes, one or both may meet new partners. Those relationships will proceed with more success if not bogged down by old baggage.

A variety of research indicates that initially after a divorce, life satisfaction drops. Although many people report feeling relief as they are freed from old interactions and concerns, they also feel stress about adjusting to their new lives. Men tend to feel less satisfaction with family life, while for women, financial concerns are the most troubling. But both men and women adapt over time, and happiness is likely to rise for both after five years, especially if they have found a new relationship. Men are much more likely to remarry than women at this stage of life.

But some long-standing couples separate but don't bother to divorce. Some make the situation work by living apart together; they remain a couple but live apart. Other couples who separate but don't bother to divorce live separately but manage their finances together, keeping their assets in the family, which can benefit both themselves and their children. Often, there is an agreement that they can each date and even get into a serious relationship, and unless one of them finds someone they really want to marry, the original couple won't bother divorcing.

Some couples divorce but remain on such friendly terms that the people around them may be confused. Their friendship worked but their marriage didn't. They may even be best friends but no longer have a sexual spark between them.

Whatever the solution for moving on, the hope is that couples who split can work out ways to be connected and happy during this time in their lives.

Tying It All Together

Long after becoming officially separated, selling their home, and moving into separate places—as well as negotiating a financial agreement and putting the divorce process into motion—Nina and Ryan both went to Anna's holiday party. They hadn't seen or spoken to each other in months but each was doing well, walking through the emotions, and leaning on their support network of family and friends. Ryan had even gone on a few dates. Nina was thinking about dating but hadn't started yet.

They were both a bit wary about seeing each other. But when they did, they hugged and asked after each other. Both knew that even though they'd moved on, they'd always be a part of each other's lives.

Cooperative Separation and Divorce

If you and your partner are having issues that feel irreconcilable despite extensive efforts, you may want to try following our advice in this section because working out a peaceful separation is important not only to you and your partner, but to all the people who care about you both. If you want to try to improve your ability to cooperate and meet the needs of both of you as you work through your separation and divorce, here is what we recommend:

Read over the "Tips for Talking and Listening" found at the beginning of this book. Then sit down for a conversation and take turns telling each other how you feel about your separation and divorce, sharing your concerns and your worries about the future. Let yourselves be vulnerable. Do your best to listen patiently, quietly, and nonjudgmentally. Give your partner time to talk. Remember that this isn't easy for either of you.

Respond with a validating comment when you each can, even if what you are hearing is surprising or upsetting. Be respectful and supportive. You aren't solving problems now; you are sharing feelings and learning about each other's needs and wishes.

Remember that your goal is to make this process as peaceful, equitable, and caring as possible. Try to set a positive goal, one in which you can each support the other as you move forward together and apart.

A Week Later

About a week later, spend another hour in the same way, discussing areas of agreement and disagreement. Make a plan to spend time together again as often as you need to, hammering out the details of particular issues. Try to take each of your separate interests into account. Imagine being in each other's shoes.

Here are some questions to spur your conversation:

- What will each of you miss from the relationship?
- What are some of your favorite memories?

- What positive traits do you appreciate in each other?

- What do each of you need emotionally and financially?

- Should you use a mediator?

- Do you need a divorce counselor?

- Should you include your adult children in the conversations?

- How can you talk about finances without causing emotional distress?

- How should you handle significant life events, such as graduations and weddings?

- How will your relationship look in the future?

- Can you be friends?

- What happens to your mutual friendships with other couples?

- How will each of you feel if one of you remarries?

- Can you maintain care and compassion for each other to honor the years you had together?

Try to keep in mind that you've had years together and you've cared about each other even though you may have hurt or disappointed each other. Focus on the present and future and avoid delving into past conflicts as you consider together how you want your lives to be going forward. Remember to consider family and friends as you plan together.

If the process becomes tense, take a break. Don't let strong feelings that may arise interfere with your mission to make this separation or divorce as amicable as possible. Everyone has intense feelings. Don't judge whether they are right or wrong, valid or not, real or fictive. Just let each other feel, try to be accepting, and move on. If that isn't enough to manage the feelings, walk away, calm down, try to take the long view, and refocus on the goal. Return to your process when you are both ready. Get professional help when you need it.

Take your time. You've had a long relationship. Change can be painful and challenging. You aren't ending the relationship altogether, even if you are getting divorced; you're changing it to meet changing needs in one or both of you. Acknowledge the loss, appreciate each other's efforts, and remember that you will both be better off if you can cooperate and part ways as friends.

An Ongoing Plan to Integrate Change

Try to be accepting and respectful as you continue to work on the big changes in your lives. Your goal is to feel more peacefully connected as you plan to separate. Even as you continue to work on areas about which you disagree, try to share feelings, remember positive experiences, and aim for compromise and understanding. Avoid revisiting old hurts and negative incidents. Those are in the past and won't help you as you create a new path forward. You've known each other for a long time. You have family and friends who will be affected by your choices. Even if you don't belong together forever, you can support each other as you move forward into your new life experiences.

Steps to Success

As you and your partner work to part ways, you should each have the best opportunity to move on well, to seek a relationship with a better fit if desired and a future with the possibility of peace and happiness. Holding on to spite and resentment only leads to more bitterness. Remember that life isn't fair and dwelling in anger doesn't lead to joy.

- Compromise and cooperate when necessary. Remember that it benefits others.

- Communicate about your vision for the future.

- Try to let go and move on while having the humility to acknowledge that you are both flawed humans. That is the key to a successful conclusion to your marriage. This acceptance will allow both of you to remain engaged with family and friends and even each other in new ways if desired.

- Forgive yourselves and each other.

The goal is to move forward with your lives in peace and to find happiness.

Afterword

Final Thoughts

Overheard at the supermarket: "She left him the same month their kids moved out. Can you believe it?"

Overheard at the theater: "Over here, my love." (A man said this tenderly to his wife as she came out of the restroom, searching for him in the crowd.)

Stories of remarkable spouses over fifty surround us. Some catch us by surprise because we never suspected they were having problems at all. Others inspire us with their longevity—forty, fifty, even sixty contented years together.

Most of us fall somewhere in between. We don't bolt, but we're not perennially happy. We have good times and bad, periods of ease and struggle. We hope to bring out the best in our partner, and we hope our partner brings out the best in us. We hope for understanding, a sanctuary from our hectic worlds, warm companionship, and shared laughter. But as this book has shown, there are always challenges to face and essential conversations to have.

One of the privileges of being a psychotherapist is to help couples squarely face those difficulties and have those emotionally charged conversations. When partners can hear the hurt in each other's voices and understand each other's vulnerabilities and needs, they can grow through adversity. They can renew their commitment to each other while adapting their relationship to the changes that come with age. They can learn to love in different ways.

We hope that with the help of this book, you are more able to together face the challenges in your relationship, to work through them to create a more intimate, positive connection. We know it's easy to blame or avoid each other in tough times, rather than turn toward each other to face the pain and grow together. We also know that as time passes, old challenges fade and new ones appear. We hope that you'll put this book on your nightstand and use it as a resource to return to when difficulties arise. We also hope that you will stand together as a team and face issues together, growing stronger with each challenge.

This phase of life can be one of a renewed pursuit of happiness. You can make it a joyous one as you focus on each other, grow to increasingly appreciate the valuable connection you have, and continue to share experiences and inspiration.

Acknowledgments

To the many clients who have shared your stories with us, enlightened us, humbled us, and allowed us to join you in your efforts to love and care for each other more deeply. We feel honored to include some of your experiences in this book.

To our family, friends, and neighbors who have candidly shared your relationship struggles and successes with us, some of which are in this book, and who have been there for us through the long writing process. Thank you. Your support means so much.

To Monica and Aaron, who have been unceasingly supportive and caring. Thank you for being there for us and for being who you are. We love you.

To Barry's colleagues at Health Management Associates, a great healthcare consulting firm. He has been uplifted by your belief in the power of relationships to change the world.

To Jodi Lipson. This book would not exist without you. Your creative ideas, incisive editing, and tireless encouragement have carried us through the entire process.

To Tom Miller with Liza Dawson Associates. Thank you for moving the book along so seamlessly from start to finish and for providing thoughtful suggestions and feedback all along the way.

To Dan Ambrosio. Thank you for your encouragement and feedback and for helping us make this book a reality.

We are so grateful to have had the opportunity to work with Dan, Tom, and Jodi, a stellar team of experts, once again.

Notes

The Empty Nest

Bouchard, G. (2018). A dyadic examination of marital quality at the empty-nest phase. *International Journal of Aging and Human Development*, 86(1): 34–50. https://journals.sagepub.com/doi/abs/10.1177/0091415017691285

Kulik, L. (2016). Spousal role allocation and equity in older couples. In *Couple Relationships in the Middle and Later Years—Their Nature, Complexity, and Role in Health and Illness* (ed. J. Bookwala), 138–139. Washington, DC: APA Books.

Lu, X. L., et al. (2013). Short form 36-Item Health Survey test result on the empty nest elderly in China: A meta-analysis. *Archives of Gerontology and Geriatrics*, 56(2): 291–297. https://www.ncbi.nlm.nih.gov/pubmed/23182316

McCullough, P. G., and Rutenberg, S. K. (1988). Launching children and moving on. In *Changing Family Life Cycle*, 2nd ed. (eds. B. Carter and M. McGoldrick), 285–309. New York: Gardner Press. http://healingreligion.com/PS1012/html/launching_children_and_moving_on.htm

Polenick, C. A. (2018). Parental support of adult children and middle-aged couples' marital satisfaction. *The Gerontologist*, 58(4): 663–673. https://www.ncbi.nlm.nih.gov/pmc/articles/PMC6044335/

Polenick, C. A., et al. (2018). Relationship quality with parents: Implications for own and partner well-being in middle-aged couples. *Family Process, 57*(1): 253–268. https://www.ncbi.nlm.nih.gov/pmc/articles/PMC5481501/

Extended Family

American Psychological Association. (n.d.). Marriage and divorce. http://www.apa.org/topics/divorce/

Aranda, L. (2015). Doubling-up: A gift or a shame? Intergenerational households and parental depression of older Europeans. *Social Science & Medicine, 134*: 12–22. http://www.sciencedirect.com/science/article/abs/pii/S0277953 615002099

Bushnell, M. (2015). Study: Boomerang children hurt boomers' retirement prospects. American Society of Pension Professionals & Actuaries, March 17. http://www.asppa.org/news-resources/browse-topics/study-boomerang -children-hurt-boomers%E2%80%99-retirement-prospects

Casares, D. R., Jr., and White, C. C. (2018). The phenomenological experience of parents who live with a boomerang child. *American Journal of Family Therapy, 46*(3): 227–243. http://www.tandfonline.com/doi/abs/10.1080/01926187.2 018.1495133

Courtin, E., and Avendano, M. (2016). Under one roof: The effect of co-residing with adult children on depression in later life. *Social Science & Medicine, 168*: 140–149. https://www.ncbi.nlm.nih.gov/pubmed/27654932

Fry, R. (2015). More millennials living with family despite improved job market. Pew Research Center, July 29. http://www.pewsocialtrends.org/2015 /07/29/more-millennials-living-with-family-despite-improved-job-market/

Houle, J., and Warner, C. (2017). Into the red and back to the nest? Student debt, college completion, and returning to the parental home among young adults. *Sociology of Education, 90*(1): 89–108. https://journals.sagepub.com /doi/full/10.1177/0038040716685873

Jensen, B. (2015). What to do about your boomerang kid. AARP Home & Family, June 19. http://www.aarp.org/home-family/friends-family/info-2017 /what-makes-a-family-a-family.html

Papernow, P. L. (2018). Clinical guidelines for working with stepfamilies: What every family, couple, individual, and child therapist needs to know. *Family Process*, 57(1): 25–51. https://www.ncbi.nlm.nih.gov/pubmed/29057461

Papernow, P. L. (2018). Recoupling in mid-life and beyond: From love at last to not so fast. *Family Process*, 57(1): 52–69. https://www.ncbi.nlm.nih.gov /pubmed/28887892

Pew Research Center. (2015). Parenting in America. December 17. http:// www.pewsocialtrends.org/2015/12/17/1-the-american-family-today/

Tosi, M., and Grundy, E. (2018). Returns home by children and changes in parents' well-being in Europe. *Social Science & Medicine* (March): 99–106. http:// www.sciencedirect.com/science/article/pii/S0277953618300169

Wood, J. (2018). The United States divorce rate is dropping, thanks to millennials. World Economic Forum, October 5. http://www.weforum.org /agenda/2018/10/divorce-united-states-dropping-because-millennials/

Finances

AARP. (2014). Budgeting worksheet. August. http://www.aarp.org/content /dam/aarp/money/budgeting_savings/2014-08/budgeting-worksheet -aarp.pdf

Barton, A. W., and Bryant, C. M. (2016). Financial strain, trajectories of marital processes, and African American newlyweds' marital instability. *Journal of Family Psychology*, 30(6): 657–664. https://www.ncbi.nlm.nih.gov/pmc/articles /PMC5014652/

Consumer.gov. (n.d.). Making a budget. http://www.consumer.gov/articles /1002-making-budget#!what-to-do

Cubanski, J., et al. (2018). How many seniors live in poverty? Kaiser Family Foundation, November 19. http://www.kff.org/medicare/issue-brief/how -many-seniors-live-in-poverty/

Cussen, M. (2019). Problems faced by senior citizens and the elderly. Mason Finance, April 26. http://www.masonfinance.com/blog/problems-of-elderly/

Gibson, W. E. (2019). Nearly half of Americans 55+ have no retirement savings or benefits. AARP, March 28. http://www.aarp.org/retirement/retirement -savings/info-2019/no-retirement-money-saved.html

GoodTherapy. (2019). Control issues. August 26. http://www.goodtherapy .org/learn-about-therapy/issues/control-issues

Johnson, J. (2016). The biggest financial worries for middle-aged Americans. *Forbes*, June 1. http://www.forbes.com/sites/joeljohnson/2016/06/01/concerns -of-middle-aged-americans/#71c1b5c75796

Khalfani-Cox, L. (2012). Managing marriage and money issues. AARP Money, May. http://www.aarp.org/money/investing/info-05-2012/marriage -and-money-issues.html

Merrill Lynch 2014 Report: Work and retirement: Myths and motivations. Age Wave, July 2016. https://agewave.com/wp-content/uploads/2016/07/2014 -ML-AW-Work-in-Retirement_Myths-and-Motivations.pdf

Payoff.com. (n.d.). 5 simple steps to create a successful budget. http://www .payoff.com/life/money/5-simple-steps-to-create-a-successful-budget/

Sagon, C. (2016). Drug costs for older adults still soaring. AARP Health. http:// www.aarp.org/health/drugs-supplements/info-2016/drug-costs-for-older -adults-still-soaring-cs.html

Schwain, L. (2019). What is a budget? NerdWallet, January 31. http://www .nerdwallet.com/blog/finance/what-is-a-budget/

Infidelity

Brody, J. E. (2018). When a partner cheats. *New York Times*, January 22. http:// www.nytimes.com/2018/01/22/well/marriage-cheating-infidelity.html

Fitzgerald, J., ed. (2017). *Foundations for Couples' Therapy: Research for the Real World*. New York: Routledge. https://doi.org/10.4324/9781315678610

Glass, S. P., and Wright, T. L. (1992). Justifications for extramarital relationships: The association between attitudes, behaviors, and gender. *Journal of Sex Research*, 29(3): 361–387. https://psycnet.apa.org/record/1993-05474-001

Grande, D. (2017). Couples therapy: Does it really work? *Psychology Today*, December 6. http://www.psychologytoday.com/us/blog/in-it-together/201712/couples-therapy-does-it-really-work

Lalasz, C. B., and Weigel, D. J. (2011). Understanding the relationship between gender and extradyadic relations: The mediating role of sensation seeking on intentions to engage in sexual infidelity. *Personality and Individual Differences*, 50(7): 1079–1083. http://www.sciencedirect.com/science/article/abs/pii/S019188691100050X

Marin, R. A., Christensen, A., and Atkins, D. C. (2014). Infidelity and behavioral couple therapy: Relationship outcomes over 5 years following therapy. *Couple and Family Psychology: Research and Practice*, 3(1): 1–12. https://www.apa.org/pubs/journals/features/cfp-0000012.pdf

Mark, K. P., et al. (2011). Infidelity in heterosexual couples: Demographic, interpersonal, and personality-related predictors of extradyadic sex. *Archives of Sexual Behavior*, 40(5): 971–982. https://www.ncbi.nlm.nih.gov/pubmed/21667234

Perel, E. (2017). Why happy people cheat. *The Atlantic*, October. http://www.theatlantic.com/magazine/archive/2017/10/why-happy-people-cheat/537882

Stritof, S. (2019). Causes and risks of why married people cheat. Verywell Mind, November 26. http://verywellmind.com/why-married-people-cheat-2300656

Wang, W. (2018). Who cheats more? The demographics of infidelity in America. Institute for Family Studies, January 10. https://ifstudies.org/blog/who-cheats-more-the-demographics-of-cheating-in-america

Weiss, R. (2017). Should you tell your partner you cheated? *Psychology Today*, June 9. http://www.psychologytoday.com/us/blog/love-and-sex-in-the-digital-age/201706/should-you-tell-your-partner-you-cheated

Retirement

AARP. (2019). Many expect their retirement assets to be insufficient, says AARP survey. April 25. https://press.aarp.org/2019-4-25-Retirement-Assets -Insufficient-AARP-Survey

Ameriprise Financial. (2015). Ameriprise study: First wave of baby boomers say health and emotional preparation are keys to a successful retirement. February 3. https://newsroom.ameriprise.com/archive/news-releases-archive /ameriprise-study-first-wave-baby-boomers-say-health-and-emotional -preparation-are-keys-to-successful-retirement.htm

Ameriprise Financial. (2016). Pay yourself in retirement: Research report. February. http://www.ameriprise.com/cm/groups/public/documents/document /p-035279.pdf

Chen, W.-H. (2019). Health and transitions into nonemployment and early retirement among older workers in Canada. *Economics and Human Biology*, 35(December): 193–206. http://www.sciencedirect.com/science/article/pii /S1570677X1830371X

Curl, A., and Townsend, A. L. (2013). A multilevel dyadic study of the impact of retirement on self-rated health: Does retirement predict worse health in married couples? *Research on Aging*, March. http://www.researchgate.net /publication/255729694

Genoe, M. R., et al. (2018). Retirement transitions among baby boomers: Findings from an online qualitative study. *Canadian Journal on Aging*, 37(4): 450–463. http://www.cambridge.org/core/journals/canadian-journal-on-aging -la-revue-canadienne-du-vieillissement/article/retirement-transitions-among -baby-boomers-findings-from-an-online-qualitative-study/EAFB1DC6F0579 601DF211540409B6ABD

Goodman, M. (2013). How to avoid living unhappily ever after in retirement. Next Avenue, March 6. http://www.nextavenue.org/how-avoid-living -unhappily-ever-after-retirement/

Heaven, B., et al. (2013). Supporting well-being in retirement through meaningful social roles: Systematic review of intervention studies. *Milbank Quarterly*, 91(2): 222–287. https://www.ncbi.nlm.nih.gov/pmc/articles/PMC3696198/

Hellmich, N. (2015). Retired baby boomers face emotional adjustments. *Courier Journal*, February 4. http://www.courier-journal.com/story/life/2015/02/04/baby-boomers-retirement-emotional/22857275/

Hughes, D. (2017). 10 tips to help your marriage survive retirement. *U.S. News & World Report*, March 30. https://money.usnews.com/money/blogs/on-retirement/articles/2017-03-30/10-tips-to-help-your-marriage-survive-retirement

Karpen, R. R. (2017). Reflections on women's retirement. *The Gerontologist*, 57(1): 103–109. https://academic.oup.com/gerontologist/article/57/1/103/2632092

Keck, K. (2007). Emotional changes of retirement can tarnish golden years. CNN, January 9. http://www.cnn.com/2007/US/01/09/law.emotional/index.html

Kirkpatrick, D. (2019). Reasons to live: Finding your purpose after retirement or financial independence. Can I Retire Yet?, April 1. http://www.caniretireyet.com/reasons-to-live-finding-your-purpose-after-retirement-or-financial-independence/

Michinov, E., et al. (2008). Retirees' social identity and satisfaction with retirement. *International Journal of Aging and Human Development* (March 11). https://journals.sagepub.com/doi/abs/10.2190/AG.66.3.a

Oppong, T. (2018). Your life will be incredibly better if you pursue meaning instead of happiness. Medium, January 16. https://medium.com/thrive-global/this-year-pursue-meaning-instead-of-happiness-71e1bb3a3d8f

Robertson, K. (2018). Why the world needs to rethink retirement. *New York Times*, December 4. http://www.nytimes.com/2018/12/30/business/retirement/why-the-world-needs-to-rethink-retirement.html

Rudden, J. (2020). Number of retired workers receiving Social Security in the United States from 2009 to 2019. Statista, January 6. http://www.statista.com/statistics/194295/number-of-us-retired-workers-who-receive-social-security/

Segel-Karpas, D., et al. (2013). Income decline and retiree well-being: The moderating role of attachment. *Psychology and Aging*, 28(4): 1098–1107. https://psycnet.apa.org/record/2013-44002-014

Siguaw, J. A., et al. (2017). Biopsychosocial and retirement factors influencing satisfaction with life: New perspectives. *International Journal of Aging and Human Development*, 85(4): 332–353. https://www.ncbi.nlm.nih.gov/pubmed/28042717

Downsizing and Relocating

AARP Bulletin. (n.d.). If you lived here, you'd be happy now. http://www.aarp.org/home-family/your-home/info-2015/best-places-to-live-retire.html#slide1

Age Wave. (n.d.). Finances in retirement: New challenges, new solutions [summary of the Merrill Lynch report]. http://agewave.com/what-we-do/landmark-research-and-consulting/research-studies/finances-in-retirement-new-challenges-new-solutions/

Ambrose, E. (2015). Selling your home. AARP Money, August/September. http://www.aarp.org/money/investing/info-2015/downsize-home-for-retirement.html

Burbank, J., and Keely, L. (2015). Uncommon sense: Most baby boomers are not downsizing (quite the contrary). Nielsen, January 9. http://www.nielsen.com/us/en/insights/article/2015/most-baby-boomers-are-not-downsizing-quite-the-contrary/

CityStash. (n.d.). Infographic: The upside of downsizing. Senior Lifestyle. http://www.seniorlifestyle.com/infographic-upside-downsizing/

CRES Insurance. (2016). Baby boomer real estate trends: They will surprise you. October 12. http://www.cresinsurance.com/baby-boomer-real-estate-trends-they-will-surprise-you/

Ekerdt, D. J., and Sergeant, J. F. (2006). Family things: Attending the household disbandment of older adults. *Journal of Aging Studies*, 20(3): 193–205. https://www.ncbi.nlm.nih.gov/pubmed/17047729

Ekerdt, D. J., et al. (2004). Household disbandment in later life. *Journals of Gerontology, Series B: Psychological Sciences and Social Sciences*, 59(5): S265–S273. https://www.ncbi.nlm.nih.gov/pubmed/15358801

Ekerdt, D. J., et al. (2012). Safe passage of goods and self during residential relocation in later life. *Ageing & Society,* 32(5): 833–850. https://www.ncbi.nlm .nih.gov/pubmed/23761946

Harvard Health Publishing. (2018). Tips to cope when it's time to downsize. September. http://www.health.harvard.edu/mind-and-mood/tips-to-cope-when -its-time-to-downsize

Jameson, M. (2016). *Downsizing the Family Home: What to Save, What to Let Go.* New York: Sterling.

Kaysen, R. (2019). How to sell, donate or recycle your stuff. *New York Times,* January 11. http://www.nytimes.com/2019/01/11/realestate/how-to-sell -donate-or-recycle-your-stuff.html

Kulp, K. (2016). How to know when downsizing your home makes sense. Age Wave, August 28. http://agewave.com/wp-content/uploads/2016/08 /08-28-16-CNBC_-How-to-know-when-downsizing.pdf

Merrill Lynch/Bank of America. (2019). Finances in retirement: New challenges, new solutions. https://www.benefitplans.baml.com/publish/content /application/pdf/GWMOL/2019_Finance_Study.pdf

MyMove. (2019). Senior-friendly guide to downsizing. June 26. https:// mymove.com/moving/senior-guide-downsizing/

Platsky, J. (2018). Ready to downsize? These are the biggest things to keep in mind. Press Connects, August 22. http://www.pressconnects.com/story /news/2018/08/22/downsizing-common-strategy-older-homeowners /673084002/

Rae, D. (2018). 8 questions to help you decide whether to move in retirement. *Forbes,* October 10. http://www.forbes.com/sites/davidrae/2018/10/10/move -in-retirement/#395cda484ef4

Ranada, Å. L., and Hagberg, J.-E. (2014). All the things I have: Handling one's material room in old age. *Journal of Aging Studies, 31*(December): 110–118. http://www.sciencedirect.com/science/article/abs/pii/S0890406 514000553

Schwartz, S. (2015). Relocating in retirement? Experts say look before leaping. CNBC, September 16. http://www.cnbc.com/2015/09/16/relocating-in -retirement-experts-say-look-before-leaping.html

Sex

Araki, C. (2005). Sexuality of aging couples—from women's point of view [article in Japanese]. *Acta Urologica Japonica*, 51(9): 591–594. https://repository .kulib.kyoto-u.ac.jp/dspace/handle/2433/113685

Chapman, G. (2015). *The 5 Love Languages: The Secret to Love That Lasts.* Chicago: Northfield.

Degauguier, C., et al. (2012). Impact of aging on sexuality [article in French]. *Revue Medicale de Bruxelles,* 33(3): 153–163. https://www.ncbi.nlm.nih.gov /pubmed/22891587

Fileborn, B., et al. (2015). Sex, desire and pleasure: Considering the experiences of older Australian women. *Sexual and Relationship Therapy,* 30(1): 117–130. https://www.ncbi.nlm.nih.gov/pmc/articles/PMC4270421/

Fisher, L. L., et al. (2010). Sex, romance, and relationships: AARP survey of midlife and older adults. AARP, May. http://www.aarp.org/content/dam /aarp/research/surveys_statistics/general/2011/sex-romance-relationships -09.doi.10.26419%252Fres.00063.001.pdf

Fisher, W. A., et al. (2014). Individual and partner correlates of sexual satisfaction and relationship happiness in midlife couples: Dyadic analysis of the international survey of relationships. *Archives of Sexual Behavior,* 44(6): 1609–1620. https://link.springer.com/article/10.1007%2Fs10508-014-0426-8

Flynn, K. E., et al. (2016). Sexual satisfaction and the importance of sexual health to quality of life throughout the life course of US adults. *Journal of Sexual Medicine,* 13(11): 1642–1650. https://www.ncbi.nlm.nih.gov/pmc/articles /PMC5075511/

Galinsky, A. M., and Waite, L. J. (2014). Sexual activity and psychological health as mediators of the relationship between physical health and marital quality.

Journals of Gerontology, Series B: Psychological Sciences and Social Sciences, 69(3): 482–492. https://www.ncbi.nlm.nih.gov/pmc/articles/PMC3983915/

Gaspard, T. (2016). 10 ways to rekindle the passion in your marriage. Gottman Institute, December 7. http://www.gottman.com/blog/10-ways-rekindle -passion-marriage/

Ginsberg, T. B. (2006). Aging and sexuality. *Medical Clinics of North America,* 90(5): 1025–1036. http://www.sciencedirect.com/science/article/abs/pii /S0025712506000605

Gottman, John. (2017). Building a great sex life is not rocket science. Gottman Institute, January 4. https://www.gottman.com/blog/building-great-sex -life-not-rocket-science/

Harvard Health Publishing. (2017). Attitudes about sexuality and aging. March 17. http://www.health.harvard.edu/staying-healthy/attitudes-about-sexuality -and-aging

Harvard Health Publishing. (2006). Life after 50: A Harvard study of male sexuality. March. http://www.health.harvard.edu/newsletter_article/Life_after _50_A_Harvard_study_of_male_sexuality

Howard, J. R., et al. (2006). Factors affecting sexuality in older Australian women: Sexual interest, sexual arousal, relationships and sexual distress in older Australian women. *Climacteric,* 9(5): 355–367. http://www.tandfonline.com /doi/abs/10.1080/13697130600961870

Live Bold & Bloom. (n.d.). 23 of the best relationship goals to nurture intimacy. https://liveboldandbloom.com/02/relationships/relationship-goals

McCarthy, B. W. (2012). Shifting gears: The five dimensions of touch. *Psychology Today,* May 15. http://www.psychologytoday.com/us/blog/whats-your -sexual-style/201205/shifting-gears

Northrup, C., et al. (n.d.). Sex at 50-plus: What's normal? AARP Home & Family.http://www.aarp.org/home-family/sex-intimacy/info-01-2013/seniors -having-sex-older-couples.html

Rehman, U. S., et al. (2011). The importance of sexual self-disclosure to sexual satisfaction and functioning in committed relationships. *Journal of Sexual*

Medicine, 8(11): 3108–3115. http://www.jsm.jsexmed.org/article/S1743-6095 (15)33335-X/fulltext

Ribes, G., and Cour, F. (2013). Sexuality of the elderly: A survey and management [article in French]. *Progrès en Urologie,* 23(9): 752–760. https://www.ncbi.nlm.nih.gov/pubmed/23830270

Seisen, T., et al. (2012). Influence of aging on male sexual health [article in French]. *Progrès en Urologie,* 22(suppl. 1): S7–S13. http://www.sciencedirect.com/science/article/pii/S1166708712700295

Waite, L. J., et al. (2017). Sexuality in older couples: Individual and dyadic characteristics. *Archives of Sexual Behavior,* 46(2): 605–618. https://www.ncbi.nlm.nih.gov/pmc/articles/PMC5554590/

Waldbieser, J. (2019). Why women need to talk about midlife sex—a lot. AARP, November 27. http://www.aarp.org/disrupt-aging/stories/info-2019/sex-after-menopause.html

WebMD. (n.d.). 7 tips for better sex after 50. http://www.webmd.com/healthy-aging/guide/sex-after-50#1

Health Concerns

Beard, J. R., et al. (2016). The World report on ageing and health: A policy framework for healthy ageing. *The Lancet,* 387(10033): 2145–2154. https://www.ncbi.nlm.nih.gov/pmc/articles/PMC4848186/

Beard, J. R., et al. (2016). The World report on ageing and health. *The Gerontologist,* 56(suppl. 2): S163–S166. https://academic.oup.com/gerontologist/article/56/Suppl_2/S163/2605374

Bernstein, L. (2015). In sickness and health: Wife's serious illness increases chance of divorce later in life; husband's doesn't. *Washington Post,* March 6. http://www.washingtonpost.com/news/to-your-health/wp/2015/03/06/in-sickness-and-health-wifes-serious-illness-increases-chance-of-divorce-later-in-life-husbands-doesnt/

Bookwala, J. (2014). Spouse health status, depressed affect, and resilience in mid and late life: A longitudinal study. *Developmental Psychology, 50*(4): 1241–1249. https://www.ncbi.nlm.nih.gov/pubmed/24364828

Clouston, S. A., et al. (2014). The role of partnership status on late-life physical function. *Canadian Journal on Aging, 33*(4): 413–425. https://www.ncbi.nlm.nih.gov/pubmed/25222477

Dailey, R. M., et al. (2011). Confirmation in couples' communication about weight management: An analysis of how both partners contribute to individuals' health behaviors and conversational outcomes. *Human Communication Research, 37*(4): 553–582. https://academic.oup.com/hcr/article-abstract/37/4/553/4107528

Fässberg, M. M., et al. (2015). A systematic review of physical illness, functional disability, and suicidal behaviour among older adults. *Aging & Mental Health, 20*(2): 166–194. http://www.tandfonline.com/doi/full/10.1080/13607863.2015.1083945

Haase, C. M. (2016). Interpersonal emotional behaviors and physical health: A 20-year longitudinal study of long-term married couples. *Emotion, 16*(7): 965–977. https://www.ncbi.nlm.nih.gov/pubmed/27213730

Holt-Lunstad, J., et al. (2017). Advancing social connection as a public health priority in the United States. *American Psychologist, 72*(6): 517–530. https://www.ncbi.nlm.nih.gov/pubmed/28880099

Karraker, A., and Latham, K. (2015). In sickness and in health? Physical illness as a risk factor for marital dissolution in later life. *Journal of Health and Social Behavior, 56*(3): 420–435. https://www.ncbi.nlm.nih.gov/pubmed/26315504

Kiecolt-Glaser, J. K., and Newton, T. L. (2001). Marriage and health: His and hers. *Psychological Bulletin, 127*(4): 472–503. https://psycnet.apa.org/record/2001-01085-002

Kim, Y. et al. (2018). Aging together: Self-perceptions of aging and family experiences among Korean baby boomer couples. *The Gerontologist, 58*(6): 1044–1053. https://academic.oup.com/gerontologist/article-abstract/58/6/1044/4085776

Li, K.-K., et al. (2013). Concordance of physical activity trajectories among middle-aged and older married couples: Impact of diseases and functional difficulties. *Journals of Gerontology, Series B: Psychological Sciences and Social Sciences*, 68(5): 794–806. https://academic.oup.com/psychsocgerontology /article/68/5/794/596353

Mejia, S. T, and Gonzalez, R. (2017). Couples' shared beliefs about aging and implications for future functional limitations. *The Gerontologist*, 57(suppl. 2): S149–S159. https://www.ncbi.nlm.nih.gov/pmc/articles/PMC5881752/

Meyler, D., et al. (2007). Health concordance within couples: A systematic re- view. *Social Science & Medicine*, 64(11): 2297–2310. http://www.sciencedirect .com/science/article/abs/pii/S0277953607000433

Monin, J. K., et al. (2017). Spouses' daily feelings of appreciation and self- reported well-being. *Health Psychology* 36(12): 1135–1139. https://www.ncbi .nlm.nih.gov/pubmed/28726476

National Center for Chronic Disease Prevention and Health Promotion. (2011). Healthy aging: Helping people to live long and productive lives and enjoy a good quality of life. AARP. https://www.aarp.org/content/dam/aarp/livable -communities/old-learn/health/Healthy-Aging-Helping-People-to-Live-Long -and-Productive-Lives-and-Enjoy-a-Good-Quality-of-Life-2011-AARP.pdf

National Institute on Aging (n.d.) Exercise and physical activity. https://go4life .nia.nih.gov/

Parker-Pope, T. (2010). Is marriage good for your health? *New York Times*, April 18. http://www.nytimes.com/2010/04/18/magazine/18marriage-t.html

Sagon, C. (2016). 9 ways your mate can affect your health. AARP Health, October. http://www.aarp.org/health/healthy-living/info-2016/marriage-spouse -affect-health-cs.html

Shmerling, R. H. (2016). The health advantages of marriage. Harvard Health Publishing, November 30. http://www.health.harvard.edu/blog/the-health -advantages-of-marriage-2016113010667

Siegel, M. J., et al. (2004). The effect of spousal mental and physical health on husbands' and wives' depressive symptoms, among older adults: Longitudinal evidence from the Health and Retirement Survey. *Journal of Aging and Health*,

16(3): 398–425. https://journals.sagepub.com/doi/abs/10.1177/0898264
304264208

Thomas, S. N. (2015). Prescription for living longer: Spend less time
alone. Brigham Young University, March 10. https://news.byu.edu/news
/prescription-living-longer-spend-less-time-alone

Traa, M. J., et al. (2015). Dyadic coping and relationship functioning in couples coping with cancer: A systematic review. *British Journal of Health Psychology,*
20(1): 85–114. https://onlinelibrary.wiley.com/doi/abs/10.1111/bjhp.12094

Walker, R. B., and Luszcz, M. A. (2009). The health and relationship dynamics of
late-life couples: A systematic review of the literature. *Ageing & Society, 29*(3): 455–
480. http://www.cambridge.org/core/journals/ageing-and-society/article/health
-and-relationship-dynamics-of-latelife-couples-a-systematic-review-of-the-literature
/C0EA01D96D544A95B75374D3BE882E19

Caregiving

Adler, S. E. (2019). Family caregivers provide billions of hours of care annu-
ally. AARP Family Caregiving, November 14. http://www.aarp.org/caregiving
/financial-legal/info-2019/family-caregiver-contribution-study.html

American Psychological Association. (n.d.). Psychologists as educators. http://
www.apa.org/pi/about/publications/caregivers/education/psychologists

Autio, T., and Rissanen, S. (2017). Positive emotions in caring for a spouse:
A literature review. *Scandinavian Journal of Caring Sciences, 32*(1): 45–55.
https://onlinelibrary.wiley.com/doi/abs/10.1111/scs.12452

Gambini, B. (2017). Study finds the burdens of spousal caregiving alleviated by
appreciation. University at Buffalo, August 28. http://www.buffalo.edu/news
/releases/2017/08/033.html

Gaugler, J. E., and Kane, R. L., eds. (2015). *Family Caregiving in the New Normal.* London: Elsevier. http://www.elsevier.com/books/family-caregiving-in
-the-new-normal/gaugler/978-0-12-417046-9

George-Levi, S., et al. (2017). Caregiving styles and anxiety among couples: Coping versus not coping with cardiac illness. *Anxiety, Stress, and Coping, 30*(1): 107–120. https://www.ncbi.nlm.nih.gov/pubmed/27376169

Goyer, A. (2017). Joy in caregiving. AARP Family Caregiving, March 8. http://www.aarp.org/caregiving/life-balance/info-2017/joy-of-caregiving-ag.html

Juntunen, K., et al. (2018). Perceived burden among spouse, adult child, and parent caregivers. *Journal of Advanced Nursing, 74*(10): 2340–2350. https://www.ncbi.nlm.nih.gov/pubmed/29869807

Li, Q., and Loke, A. Y. (2014). A literature review on the mutual impact of the spousal caregiver-cancer patients dyads: "communication," "reciprocal influence," and "caregiver-patient congruence." *European Journal of Oncology Nursing, 18*(1): 58–65. https://www.ncbi.nlm.nih.gov/pubmed/24100089

Li, Q., and Loke, A. Y. (2014). A systematic review of spousal couple-based intervention studies for couples coping with cancer: Direction for the development of interventions. *Psycho-oncology, 23*(7): 731–739. https://www.ncbi.nlm.nih.gov/pubmed/24723336

López-Espuela, F., et al. (2018). Critical points in the experience of spouse caregivers of patients who have suffered a stroke: A phenomenological interpretive study. *PLoS ONE, 13*(4): e0195190. https://journals.plos.org/plosone/article?id=10.1371/journal.pone.0195190

Monin, J. K., et al. (2017). Spouses' daily feelings of appreciation and self-reported well-being. *Health Psychology, 36*(12): 1135–1139. https://psycnet.apa.org/record/2017-31320-001

National Alliance for Caregiving. (n.d.). Caregiving in America. http://www.caregiving.org/research/caregivingusa/

National Alliance for Caregiving and AARP Public Policy Institute. (2015). 2015 report: Caregiving in the U.S. June. http://www.caregiving.org/wp-content/uploads/2015/05/2015_CaregivingintheUS_Final-Report-June-4_WEB.pdf

National Institute on Aging. (2017). Taking care of yourself: Tips for caregivers. May 2. http://www.nia.nih.gov/health/taking-care-yourself-tips-caregivers

Oldenkamp, M., et al. (2016). Subjective burden among spousal and adult-child informal caregivers of older adults: Results from a longitudinal cohort study. *BMC Geriatrics, 16*(1): 208. https://www.ncbi.nlm.nih.gov/pubmed/27923347

Oppong, T. (2018). Your life will be incredibly better if you pursue meaning instead of happiness. Medium, January 16. https://medium.com/thrive-global /this-year-pursue-meaning-instead-of-happiness-71e1bb3a3d8f

Polenick, C. A., and DePasquale, N. (2019). Predictors of secondary role strains among spousal caregivers of older adults with functional disability. *The Gerontologist, 59*(3): 486–498. https://www.ncbi.nlm.nih.gov/pubmed/29325105

Richardson, T. J., et al. (2013). Caregiver health: Health of caregivers of Alzheimer's and other dementia patients. *Current Psychiatry Reports, 15*: 367. https:// link.springer.com/article/10.1007%2Fs11920-013-0367-2

Rolland, J. S. (2018). *Helping Couples and Families Navigate Illness and Disability.* New York: Guilford Press.

Schulz, R., ed. (2006). *Encyclopedia of Aging,* 4th ed. New York: Springer.

Schulz, R., et al. (2009). Improving the quality of life of caregivers of persons with spinal cord injury: A randomized controlled trial. *Rehabilitation Psychology, 54*(1): 1–15. https://www.ncbi.nlm.nih.gov/pmc/articles/PMC2729464/

Loss of Loved Ones

American Psychological Association. (n.d.). Grief: Coping with the loss of your loved one. http://www.apa.org/helpcenter/grief

Anderson, C. (2015). 7 do's and don'ts for staying connected as a couple during grief. Palo Alto Online, March 10. http://www.paloaltoonline.com/blogs /p/2015/03/10/7-dos-and-donts-for-staying-connected-as-a-couple-during -grief

Bennett, K. M., et al. (2010). Loss and restoration in later life: An examination of dual process model of coping with bereavement. *Omega: Journal of Death and Dying, 61*(4): 315–332. https://journals.sagepub.com/doi/abs/10.2190 /OM.61.4.d

Bonanno, G. A., et al. (2002). Resilience to loss and chronic grief: A prospective study from preloss to 18-months postloss. *Journal of Personality and Social Psychology*, 83(5): 1150–1164. https://psycnet.apa.org/doiLanding?doi=10.1037%2F0022-3514.83.5.1150

Brody, J. E. (2018). Understanding grief. *New York Times*, January 15. http://www.nytimes.com/2018/01/15/well/live/understanding-grief.html

Center for Grief Recovery and Therapeutic Services. (n.d.). Couples therapy. https://griefcounselor.org/therapy-counseling-services/couples-counseling-therapy/

Doka, K. J. (2017). Building resilience after loss. HuffPost, September 11. http://www.huffpost.com/entry/building-resilience-after-loss_b_59b6b15fe4b0e4419674c372

Hall, C. (2014). Bereavement theory: Recent developments in our understanding of grief and bereavement. *Bereavement Care*, 33(1): 7–12. http://www.tandfonline.com/doi/full/10.1080/02682621.2014.902610

Hibberd, R. (2013). Meaning reconstruction in bereavement: Sense and significance. *Death Studies*, 37(7): 670–692. http://www.tandfonline.com/doi/abs/10.1080/07481187.2012.692453

Kim, S. H., et al. (2011). Personal strength and finding meaning in conjugally bereaved older adults: A four-year prospective analysis. *Death Studies*, 35(3): 197–218. https://www.ncbi.nlm.nih.gov/pubmed/24501843

Muthler, S. (n.d.). Surviving loss as a couple. Seleni. http://www.seleni.org/advice-support/2018/3/20/surviving-loss-as-a-couple

Neimeyer, R. A. (n.d.). Reconstructing meaning in bereavement. *Rivista di Psichiatria*. http://www.rivistadipsichiatria.it/articoli.php?archivio=yes&vol_id=1009&id=10982

Nuwer, R. (2013). Couples who share grief fare better on the long term. *Smithsonian Magazine*, February 22. http://www.smithsonianmag.com/smart-news/couples-who-share-grief-fare-better-on-the-long-term-25080025/

When Nothing Works—Cooperative Separation and Divorce

Ahrons, C. (1994). *The Good Divorce: Keeping Your Family Together When Your Marriage Comes Apart*. New York: HarperCollins.

Brown, S. L., and Lin, I.-F. (2012). The gray divorce revolution: Rising divorce among middle-aged and older adults, 1990–2010. *Journals of Gerontology, Series B: Psychological Sciences and Social Sciences, 67*(6): 731–741. https://www.ncbi.nlm.nih.gov/pmc/articles/PMC3478728/

Brown, S. L., et al. (2018). Later life marital dissolution and repartnership status: A national portrait. *Journals of Gerontology, Series B: Psychological Sciences and Social Sciences, 73*(6): 1032–1042. https://www.ncbi.nlm.nih.gov/pmc/articles/PMC6093496/

Bulanda, J. R., et al. (2016). Marital quality, marital dissolution, and mortality risk during the later life course. *Social Science & Medicine, 165*: 119–127. https://www.ncbi.nlm.nih.gov/pubmed/27509579

Collett, T. S. (2018). Being older doesn't make divorce any wiser: Families like mine fight to buck divorce trend. *USA Today*, September 6. http://www.usatoday.com/story/opinion/voices/2018/09/06/gray-divorce-elderly-couples-marriage-column/1183820002/

Crowley, J. E. (2017). Gray divorce: Explaining midlife marital splits. *Journal of Women & Aging, 31*(1): 49–72. https://ncbi.nlm.nih.gov/pubmed/29210619

Crowley, J. E. (2018). *Gray Divorce—What We Lose and Gain by Mid-Life Splits*. Oakland: University of California Press.

Gravningen, K., et al. (2017). Reported reasons for breakdown of marriage and cohabitation in Britain: Findings from the third National Survey of Sexual Attitudes and Lifestyles (Natsal-3). *PLoS ONE*, March 23. https://journals.plos.org/plosone/article?id=10.1371/journal.pone.0174129

Hammond, A. (2006). Disconnected spouses. MarriageTrac, August 17. http://www.growthtrac.com/disconnected-spouses/

Henriques, G. (2014). Why is it so hard for some men to share their feelings? *Psychology Today*, November 13. http://www.psychologytoday.com/us/blog /theory-knowledge/201411/why-is-it-so-hard-some-men-share-their-feelings

Jensen, J. F., and Rauer, A. J. (2015). Marriage work in older couples: Disclosure of marital problems to spouses and friends over time. *Journal of Family Psychology*, 29(5): 732–743. https://www.ncbi.nlm.nih.gov/pubmed/26030028

Kaslow, F. W. (1981). Divorce and divorce therapy. In *Handbook of Family Therapy*, 662–696. New York: Brunner/Mazel.

Kiecolt-Glaser, J. K. (2018). Marriage, divorce, and the immune system. *American Psychologist*, 73(9): 1098–1108. https://www.ncbi.nlm.nih.gov /pubmed/30525786

Knöpfli, B., et al. (2016). Trajectories of psychological adaptation to marital breakup after a long-term marriage. *Gerontology*, 62(5): 541–552. https://www .ncbi.nlm.nih.gov/pubmed/27071043

Koren, C. (2016). Men's vulnerability—women's resilience: From widowhood to late-life repartnering. *International Psychogeriatrics*, 28(5): 719–731. https:// www.ncbi.nlm.nih.gov/pubmed/26691683

Leopold, T. (2018). Gender differences in the consequences of divorce: A study of multiple outcomes. *Demography*, 55(3): 769–797. https://www.ncbi.nlm .nih.gov/pmc/articles/PMC5992251/

Lin, I.-F., et al. (2018). Antecedents of gray divorce: A life course perspective. *Journals of Gerontology, Series B: Psychological Sciences and Social Sciences*, 73(6): 1022–1031. https://www.ncbi.nlm.nih.gov/pmc/articles/PMC6093363/

Pain Doctor. (2018). Top 10 most stressful life events: The Holmes and Rahe Stress Scale. March 2. https://paindoctor.com/top-10-stressful-life-events -holmes-rahe-stress-scale/

Pearce, D. (n.d.). Study examines life satisfaction after gray divorce. Men's Divorce. https://mensdivorce.com/life-satisfaction-gray-divorce/

Schwartz, P. (2012). Why long-married couples split. AARP Relationships, November 12. http://www.aarp.org/relationships/love-sex/info-06-2010/naked -truth-long-term-marriages-end.html

Segal, J., et al. (2019). Dealing with a breakup or divorce. HelpGuide, June. http://www.helpguide.org/articles/grief/dealing-with-a-breakup-or-divorce .htm

Stepler, R. (2017). Led by Baby Boomers, divorce rates climb for America's 50+ population. Pew Research Center, March 9. http://www.pewresearch .org/fact-tank/2017/03/09/led-by-baby-boomers-divorce-rates-climb-for -americas-50-population/

Steverman, B. (2019). Divorce is destroying the finances of Americans over 50. Bloomberg, July 19. http://www.bloomberg.com/news/articles/2019-07-19 /divorce-destroys-finances-of-americans-over-50-studies-show

Strutt, S. (n.d.). 12 real reasons why couples drift apart over time. LovePanky. http://www.lovepanky.com/love-couch/broken-heart/reasons-why-couples -drift-apart-over-time

Index

About the Authors

Julia L. Mayer, Psy.D., and Barry J. Jacobs, Psy.D., are psychologists who have been married for thirty years. Both have been practicing with individuals and couples for nearly thirty years. They co-authored *AARP Meditations for Caregivers: Practical, Emotional, and Spiritual Support for You and Your Family* and have written articles for WebMD and HealthCentral together. They travel the country and beyond, giving talks on positive caregiving, and they have been on many radio shows and podcasts. They have two grown children.

Julia has a private practice for individual and marital therapy in Media, Pennsylvania, specializing in working with women who have histories of troubled marriages and sexual trauma and with caregivers. She cohosts the podcast *Shrinks on Third*, about psychology and social justice. She spent more than twenty years consulting to agencies that house people with chronic mental illness. She held adjunct faculty appointments at the Institute for Graduate Clinical Psychology of Widener University and was an instructor for the master's program in creative arts therapy at Hahnemann University. Julia serves as past president of the board of directors for PSCP: The Psychology Network. Prior to becoming a psychologist, Julia wrote plays and interned as an assistant to the director for a theater company in New York. Her novel, *A Fleeting State of Mind*, was published in 2014.

Barry is a clinical psychologist, family therapist, and a principal at Health Management Associates, a national healthcare consulting firm. In his practice, he specializes in individuals and couples over fifty. Barry is the author of *The Emotional Survival Guide for Caregivers: Looking After Yourself and Your Family While Helping an Aging Parent*. He is the longtime national spokesperson on family caregiving for the American Heart Association, an honorary board member of the Well Spouse Association, and a monthly columnist on family caregiving for AARP.org.